PLANTED

Planted

A Story of Creation, Community, and Calling

Written and illustrated by
LEAH KOSTAMO

Foreword by
EUGENE PETERSON

CASCADE *Books* · Eugene, Oregon

PLANTED
A Story of Creation, Calling, and Community

Passages from Scripture used in this work are from the New International Version, NIV, copyright 1973, 1978, 1984 by the New York International Bible Society. Used by permission of Zondervan Bible Publishers.

A portion of Chapter Three, "Subterranean Grace in a World of Wounds," appeared in *Green Shoots in a Time of Drought: Alternative Futures for the Church in Canada,* ed. John Bowen (Eugene, OR: Wipf and Stock, 2013). Used by permission.

Published in association with literary agent Blair Jacobson of D.C. Jacobson & Associates, LLC, an Author Management Company, www.dcjacobson.com.

Cascade Books
An Imprint of Wipf and Stock Publishers
199 W. 8th Ave., Suite 3
Eugene, OR 97401

www.wipfandstock.com

ISBN 13: 978-1-62032-708-1

Cataloguing-in-Publication data:

Kostamo, Leah.

Planted : a story of creation, calling, and community / Leah Kostamo, with a foreword by Eugene Peterson.

xvi + 160 pp. ; 23 cm. Includes bibliographical references.

ISBN 13: 978-1-62032-708-1

1. Environmental protection—Religious aspects—Christianity. 2. Human ecology—Religious aspects—Christianity. I. Title.

BT695.5 K65 2013

Manufactured in the U.S.A.

For Markku
and in memory of Frank and Dorothy Richardson

The real work of planet-saving will be small, humble, and humbling and (insofar as it involves love) pleasing and rewarding. Its jobs will be too many to count, too many to report, too many to be publicly noticed or rewarded, too small to make anyone rich or famous.

WENDELL BERRY

Contents

Foreword

WHEN I SAT DOWN to read the manuscript that became this book, I intended to read for twenty minutes and then go back to working on my own manuscript. Adrenalin had been building since I got out of bed. I was itching to continue. But there was to be no other work that day. Five hours later I turned the last page with a sense that I was participating in the remarkable story of people who ventured into seriously caring for creation in a highly unusual way—establishing an Environmental Center for the care of creation, *God's creation*. With neither money nor experience they managed to acquire ten acres of land on the Little Campbell River in the Lower Mainland of British Columbia.

Eight years later, at the time this book was written, evidence had accumulated that confirmed the authenticity of what had been taking place. This book tells the story. The Center has welcomed thousands of visitors, as well as hundreds of interns, day campers, and school kids. It has grown literally tons of organic vegetables, served thousands of meals, and conducted conservation research on a myriad of species. All of this has taken place within an intentionality of staying true to the original convictions regarding creation care, hospitality, and justice.

Not the least of the excellencies of this book is the vivid liveliness and skilled artistry of the writing itself. Writers who immerse themselves in God's creation, "God's grandeur," seem to absorb some of that very grandeur into the way they write—the rhythm of the prose, the freshness of the metaphors. As I read

Leah Kostamo's witness I found myself in the company of the likes of Henry Thoreau and John Muir, Aldo Leopold and Annie Dillard, Wendell Berry and Bill McKibben, Rick Bass and Terry Tempest Williams among many others.

This is a book full of good stories told by a good storyteller. Instead of making a pitch or sermon or propagandistic tract on creation care, Leah has woven everything into a narrative, a story with characters and movement and relationship, and Jesus. Hers is an inviting witness to firsthand immersion in this creation that is "never spent."

The grandparent Environmental Center of what is described here was begun in 1983 by Peter and Miranda Harris. Peter was an Anglican priest serving a parish in Liverpool. In the course of his priestly work he developed an interest and passion in caring for and entering into the beauties and intricacies of God's creation. He observed that a widespread disconnect had developed in contemporary Christian communities at the critical point in the Lord's prayer where we pray "on earth *as* it is in heaven"—a prayer that *heaven* gets embodied, lived out, cared for, and enjoyed on *earth*— in our neighborhoods, our wetlands, our streets, our mountains, our rivers and oceans, in the air we breathe and, yes, in the birds as we learn their names and habits.

The first Environmental Center was established by Peter and Miranda in Portugal, located at Quinta da A Rocha—farm on the rock. A Rocha (pronounced *a-raw-sha*) at present has national organizations in twenty countries on five continents.

I have been in conversation and prayer with some of the leaders of A Rocha now for more than twenty years, observing the ways in which they do their work. In an arena frequently marked by controversy and acrimony, A Rocha is cheerful, winsome, exuding gratitude. I continue to be struck by two common characteristics that are given fresh expression in this book. To begin with, modesty, a humility that permeates A Rocha culture. There is nothing grandiose about what they do—it is all local, personal, relational, hospitable. As Leah Kostamo notes in her storytelling, their Center does not have a chapel as one might expect of a

Christian organization; it has a table, an altar at which they share the food they grow. And then there is such joy. These people are not motivated by anger or fear or guilt. They are quite evidently glad to be in on even the smallest and out-of-the-way venues in which they can participate in caring for God's creation.

Maybe a major contribution this book can make in the Christian community these days is to challenge the widespread reluctance, a procrastination to embrace creation care—right now. My mother guided and motivated me in wonderful ways to embrace the entire gospel with energy and joy but with one unfortunate exception, creation. Whenever we happened to be outside under Montana skies on a clear night she would often say, "Oh Eugene, I can hardly wait to get to heaven and learn the names of all the stars." One night we were talking together at the edge of the mountain lake where my dad had built a summer cabin. The night was clear and the sky was a symphony of stars. She said it again.

I was seventeen at the time and with just a trace of adolescent impatience replied, "Mother, why wait? We can start right now. Look, that's Orion the hunter. And over there is Deneb. Do you see those two bears, Ursus Major and Ursus Minor? And you really need to make friends with the Pleiades, the seven sisters—Job mentions them."

Now she was the impatient one, shrugging me off, "I can't be bothered right now; I'll wait for heaven."

But why wait. Why not *on earth* as it is in heaven? Yes, why not?

Eugene H. Peterson
Author of *The Message*
Professor Emeritus of Spiritual Theology
Regent College, Vancouver, B.C.

Acknowledgments

THE THEME OF COMMUNITY that runs through the work of A Rocha runs also through the writing of this book. I am deeply indebted to many colleagues, friends and supporters—not only for living the history described in these pages with me, but also for helping shape the written words of that lived story into something readable.

I am grateful to Peter and Miranda Harris: first, for having the audacious vision to start a bird observatory on the Portuguese coast all those years ago; secondly, for having the courage to allow A Rocha to grow into the big, beautiful, multicultural thing it has become; finally for their cheerful companionship along the Way.

I am grateful to Loren and Mary Ruth Wilkinson who have kept the flame of creation care alive in the Christian church these past thirty years and whose friendship has shaped both my life and thinking.

A particular expression of gratitude is owed to my colleagues, past and present, who have trekked with us down the A Rocha trail in Canada and have labored faithfully and at great sacrifice. They inspire me. In rough order of appearance in A Rocha's history they are: Karin Boisclair-Joly, Patrick Lilley, Ruth DesCotes, Rick Faw, Heather Robinson, Cindy Verbeek, Jessica Brouwer, Glen Carlson, Tiina Hildebrandt, Brian Marek, Sarah Willer, Stephanie Leusink, Paul and Angela Neufeld, Henry and Elma Martens, Jay and Milissa Ewing, Susan Davies, Elizabeth McKitrick, Katie Withrow, Milissa Oaks, Sandra Baird, Steve Kroeker, Jennifer Kornelsen, Agatha Kube, Samuel Chiu, Nick and Susan Pharoah, Luke

Wilson, Paul Abell, David and Shauna Anderson, Ute Lindelauf, Matt and Roxy Humphrey, Christy and Sean Juteau, Queenie Bei, Sandra Gaglardi, Bethany and Josh Paetkau, Steven Mueller and Rob DesCotes.

Likewise I am grateful for the various "teams" of folks who keep A Rocha aloft: for the wonderful and skilled men and women who comprise our Board of Directors. Their gifts of wisdom and prayer undergird this ministry and make it work; for the team of forty or so "Kostamo staff supporters" who have prayed, given financially and literally kept food on the Kostamo table so that we could be their hands and feet in the work of creation care; and for the wider circle of A Rocha friends across North America who give of their time and finances in faithful partnership.

I stand in awe of the tenacity and generosity of Irwin and Harriet Leitz, the Neufeld family, and Henry and Elma Martens, who all, in their own ways, have dreamt dreams for their land and have taken courageous steps to make those dreams a reality.

I am grateful to those who encouraged and advised me in the writing process, particularly Denise Unrau, Deana Strom, Luci Shaw, Peter and Miranda Harris, Loren Wilkinson, and Karen Hollenbeck. Thank you to Karin Boisclair-Joly for her help with the section on the Little Campbell River in chapter four, to Melissa Ong for her reflections on A Rocha Kenya's ASSETS program included in chapter nine, and to Anne Smith for the concluding sentence in chapter eleven.

I wish to thank my literary agent Blair Jacobsen for his unwavering encouragement and his tenacity to see my manuscript arrive in the right publishing hands. I also wish to thank the good people at Wipf and Stock and my editor, Rodney Clapp, in particular for their excellent and efficient handling of this project.

Finally, I wish to acknowledge those nearest and dearest who hold me in a circle of friendship and care. Thank you to my farm-mates at Kingfisher Farm who consistently expect good will and have given so much grace when I've typed at my computer while they've pulled weeds. Thank you to my family: to my mother for taking me to Orcas Island, my father for telling such good stories, and my brother for building forts in the woods. Through these acts both my life and these pages have been shaped. I am deeply indebted to Markku's parents, Seppo and Annikki Kostamo, who together have logged more volunteer hours for A Rocha than any other couple in Canada. I honor my sister Deana, my truest friend and the wisest person I know. Her encouragement was the springboard from which this book was launched. I salute my amazing girls, Maya and Bryn, who remind me every day what it means to be truly joyful. Finally, a deep thank you to Markku, my love, who has taken me by the hand and journeyed with me to places I would have feared to have gone alone. I can't imagine a better traveling companion.

1

The Study of Home

*When we try to pick out anything by itself, we find it hitched to
everything else in the Universe.*

JOHN MUIR

I GREW UP IN Arizona. And though the arid climate of the region
conjures images of dusty roads and adobe houses frocked with
cacti, our three-bedroom rancher was, in fact, surrounded by a
lush lawn that fronted a wide, paved street. The housing development in which we lived had been carved out of a retired orange
and grapefruit orchard, requiring our yards to be bermed to contain the monthly influx of irrigation drawn from a centuries-old
canal system originally built by the Hohokam Native Americans.
With the irrigation came crayfish and even the occasional real fish.
As soon as the water started bubbling, my sister, brother, and I
ran to retrieve our inflatable toy war canoe—an ironic tribute to

the canoe-less Hohokam. We spent hours paddling around the back yard, hunting for aquatic life, splashing each other with little plastic paddles. That monthly deluge was a wonder. The rest of the year, life was dry and deserty.

But each year, for four glorious weeks, we escaped the desert. Every summer, from the time I was eight until I was eighteen, my mom shoehorned three kids and a mountain of luggage and coolers into our two-tone station wagon and made the four-day pilgrimage to Orcas Island, where my grandparents lived. (My father, who couldn't spare so much time off work, parachuted in for a week or two and then grudgingly headed back to the heat to make a living.)

Every bit of those summers was magical. The temperate rain forest of the island was a tangled green so lush it almost hurt my eyes. Parched from the previous eleven months in the desert, my sister, brother, and I gulped it down in great verdant draughts. We spent nearly every daylit moment outside, scrambling along deer trails, prying limpets off rocks to use as bait to catch rock cod, building tree houses in sturdy Douglas Firs, and, as teenagers, sitting for hours at the ocean's edge contemplating the mysterious workings of the universe.

And we came back, one by one, like a stone skipped along the Northwest coast, touching down in Seattle, the Skagit Valley, and Vancouver. This was my mother's gift—not just the days of driving —but the long-term gift of taking us to a place that each summer tethered an invisible strand to our imaginations, until one day the combined strength of those strands created an irresistible pull that would draw us back and tie us down, each one, firmly to the Pacific Coast, far from her.

Those strands were woven by Orcas, the place, but also by the people—and two people in particular: my grandparents' neighbors, Frank and Dorothy Richardson. Frank was a retired professor of ornithology who looked strikingly like Leo Tolstoy, and Dorothy was a homemaker with a graduate degree in biology and crinkly fairy godmother eyes. They both were slight and ate like birds. They also ate birds. Not just chickens and turkeys: they ate little birds.

They ate robins. Or, at least, they ate one robin. We entered their kitchen one afternoon—unannounced as usual—just as they were clearing their dishes from lunch. We were surprised by the teeny bones on their plates. In response to our bewildered expressions, they explained that a robin had flown into their car windshield while they'd been driving back from town, and, not wanting it to go to waste, they had brought it home, cooked it, and ate it.

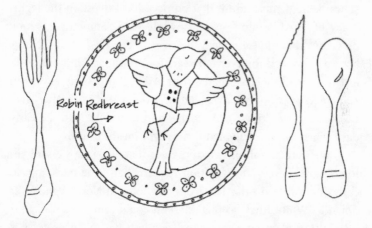

Robin Redbreast

I myself have yet to eat roadkill, but I appreciate the amazing commitment to conservation it represents. There's a First Nations-esque respect and love for creation in their unwillingness to waste what lost its life, if not at their hands, then at their windshield.

The Richardsons approached the entire natural world with this degree of care and concern. They never once sat down and lectured us on the evils of clear cuts or the plight of endangered species; they simply invited us into their lives. We caught Lingcod from their rowboat, pulled carrots in their organic garden, paddled along the coast in their hand-built kayaks, hiked along woodland trails and learned (momentarily) the Latin names for wild orchids, and when need arose used their outhouse so as not to waste the precious "indoor" water that they had collected from their rooftop.

The combination of Orcas Island's wild beauty and the Richardsons' example and friendship packed a double punch, which formed in me a deep love for creation, even the creation of my desert homeland. That love transformed into a conviction that has become an impetus for caring for creation in both my everyday and vocational life.

TRUE CONFESSIONS

But now, a confession. Despite this early grounding in creation stewardship, I must admit that on occasion I question the legitimacy of "earthkeeping" as worthwhile work. Sometimes I look down at the Little Campbell, the river in Surrey, British Columbia we've labored for over ten years to protect, and it looks, well, *little*—more like a creek than a river. And I think to myself, *Is this pathetic trickle worth all the effort!?* I think this now, after over twelve years working for A Rocha, and I thought it in the early days, when we were full of vim and vigor for the cause.

We were so full of vim and vigor that as a rule we said yes to absolutely every conservation request that came our way. An early one involved a day trip from our home in North Vancouver down to White Rock so that Markku could join a team of four people transplanting eelgrass in Boundary Bay. Now, eelgrass is important stuff—it forms the basis of a complex food web in estuaries and other shallow marine waters and provides a protective hiding place for vulnerable creatures like juvenile salmon. Though I lacked a thorough understanding of how sub-marine plant transplanting worked (I guessed, at least, that watering the seedling wouldn't be an issue) I came along for the day. I kissed scuba-clad Markku farewell at the pier and watched him descend into the very chilly Pacific waters. Two of the four divers started experiencing symptoms of hypothermia almost immediately and retreated from the ocean. That left Markku and our friend Hans to do the bulk of the work. Floundering through the murky water with a bag of sodden seedlings strapped to his side, Markku felt so constricted he could hardly move. This was not turning out to be as fun as he thought it would be. And then he saw a sailboat's keel pass just a few feet between himself and the oblivious Hans. If either of them had been in the sailboat's path they would have been knocked out.

Meanwhile I strolled along the boardwalk, pushing one child in a stroller and wearing infant Bryn in a front carrier, which I had not secured properly. The end result of my inability to properly snap up the Baby Bjorn was Bryn dropping like . . . like what? . . . a dead weight, yes, but more like a heavy helpless baby onto concrete. She landed with the most sickening thud I'd ever heard. And, naturally, her wails woke the happily slumbering Maya who chorused in with her own cries of distress, and I cursed scuba diving and eelgrass and the whole conservation endeavor all the way to the emergency room. Of course Bryn's tumble from the snuggly had nothing to do with eelgrass replanting, but somehow, irrationally, I drew a direct connection from Markku's underwater shenanigans to his lack of availability during Bryn's near-death experience. And I found myself thinking, *Is this worth it? Quitting a secure job, begging for money, selling our house and moving from our beloved community—for what? Seaweed!?!*

MAKING CONNECTIONS

The incident highlights my intermittent struggle with the importance of the whole environmental stewardship enterprise. Theologically I'm on board with the centrality of creation care to authentic Christian living, but sometimes my heart wants to perform triage on the needs of the world so I can prioritize my vocational work and financial giving accordingly. On most days malnourished African babies and AIDS sufferers in Asia go to the front of the line while the pretty fish and waving strands of eelgrass can twiddle their thumbs and wait all day to see the doctor as far as I'm concerned.

But when I perform this kind of triage I'm forgetting the principle on which all conservation is founded. I'm forgetting the fundamental definition of ecology: that everything is interconnected. I might not care about the eelgrass, but the salmon do. And the bears and blue herons need the salmon, not to mention the fisheries, and so it goes, spinning an intricate web of interwoven relationships.

A Rocha founder Peter Harris tells a story which illustrates the rippling aftershocks created when we tamper with one bit of creation's web. Apparently, the villagers in a small Peruvian hamlet got sick of the pesky bats swooping down over their huts at night, scaring their women and children. Okay, I'm embellishing; I'm sure no one, especially not the women, were afraid of those harmless bats. And hamlet sounds too romantic, but the point is, the villagers wanted the bats gone. So one morning after the bats had hung themselves up for a long day of sleep, the men of the village snuck into their cave and killed them. All. The next summer the villagers' crops were eaten up by a plague of insects, whose major predator had been eliminated by the same people who planted all those nice crops in the first place.

I'm suspicious that this story is apocryphal. I'm pretty sure those living so close to the land would be more wary about tinkering with their ecosystem, but a similar story is sadly very true. Brian Brett, in his excellent book *Trauma Farm*, recounts the devastating results of Chairman Mao's fateful Four Pests Campaign. It seems that Mao, as part of his Great Leap Forward, decided his nation would be far better off without sparrows, flies, rats, and mosquitoes. The latter three seem logical pest suspects, but sweet little House Sparrows? Evidently a sparrow can eat ten pounds of grain a year, landing it on Mao's most wanted list. Hoping to eradicate this pest from his nation, Mao instructed every citizen of China to kill sparrows on a single spring day in 1958. Over six hundred million dutiful citizens did just this—chasing sparrows from their nests and banging pots to scare them from returning, thus rendering the eggs left behind unviable. What Mao wasn't told was that while a sparrow *can* eat ten pounds of grain a year they seldom do; their diet consists mainly of insects, locusts in particular. Within two years China's crops were overrun by noxious insects, with locusts leading the assault. This, along with several other supposedly "scientific" decisions affecting farming practices, led to China's famine, which killed over twenty million people.

MAO'S LIST °F BADDIES :

1. HOUSE SPARROWS

2. FLIES

3. RATS

4. MOSQUITOES

Turns out it's not so easy to say that conservation is a luxury for citizens of wealthy nations who value hiking trails and salmon dinners, not when the survival of the world's most vulnerable people depends almost entirely on healthy ecosystems to sustain them. Again, this is where the definition of "ecology" is helpful: *eco* from the Greek *oikos*, for household, and *logia*, for "the study of." Anyone who has grown up in a household understands that it's a complicated web of interrelated relationships. (If Mama ain't happy, ain't nobody happy, right?) In essence, the word *ecology* draws attention to the relationships between living things and their environment and implies that if one tinkers with one bit of the world, the effects are felt in radiating ripples throughout the rest of the world. Tug at this thread of creation, to paraphrase John Muir, and you find it is attached to everything else. Even the smallest actions for creation care have implications for the larger web that makes up our larger home.

2

Backing into the Future

*Begin at the beginning and go on till you come
to the end: then stop.*

LEWIS CARROLL, *ALICE IN WONDERLAND*

OBVIOUSLY, MARKKU AND I didn't throw in the conservation towel when Bryn toppled from the snuggly. Nor have we given up on the Little Campbell River, though in the summer months it is reduced to creek-like proportions in places. And though we both struggle at times with the value of our work, we plod on, convinced on our better days that our vocation in the field of environmental stewardship is a calling and a privilege—convinced that matter matters to God, who created the stuff and even became the stuff and calls us to steward the stuff on his behalf.

We also try to remember the words of a wise friend who encouraged us, when faced with discouragement and tricky decisions that bring uncertain outcomes, to "back into the future." That is, we are to employ the discipline of retrospection, applying the fine white dust of memory, which reveals God's fingerprints where we might not have noticed them before. Seeing where God has led and provided in the past gives us confidence to back into the future when we feel immobilized. That's what these pages are—a way of backing into the future in order to detect God's hand in our past, that we might have courage for our future.

EARLY DAYS

Traveling back to A Rocha's beginnings in Canada isn't a long trip. Internationally, A Rocha dates back to 1982, when Peter and Miranda Harris left a thriving Anglican parish in Liverpool to start a Christian Bird Observatory (if such a beast could be started) on the coast of Portugal. Canada's chapter in the A Rocha story began in 1996 when Peter and Miranda left Portugal and, as part of a year-long sabbatical, taught a class called "Incarnational Mission" at Regent College in Vancouver.

I was in their class and readily admit to falling hopelessly in love. Their attractiveness lay not only in their winsome personalities and British accents, but in how authentically they lived out their faith. They seemed to exhibit a thorough integration of belief and life. In a nutshell, they loved God, they loved people, and they loved creation. Theology found legs in their work, friendships, and family life. For many of us, their embodiment of faith helped us shift environmental stewardship from a fringe concern to a thoroughly normal part of our Christian lives. That class, coupled with lectures presented around Vancouver, spawned the future work of A Rocha in Canada. Soon the first Board of Directors coalesced, and in 1999 A Rocha received charitable status.

While the Board was launching I was heading across the Atlantic to teach at an international university in Lithuania—an experience which proved to be very chilly, but hugely rewarding. A year and a half into my stint on the Baltic I was lured home by a marriage proposal from Markku. He likes to joke that my consent to marriage hinged upon his own consent to work for A Rocha. His version of my stance goes something like this: It was my goal in life to work for A Rocha, but having trained in the humanities, I was in need of a scientist on whose coattails I could ride into the conservation parade. Markku, an ecologist by training, was my ticket in. The truth, of course, is much more romantic—his quick smile and hearty laugh easily trumped all professional credentials! We married in 1999 and Markku joined A Rocha's fledgling Board with no coaxing from me.

Our first Board of Directors was quintessentially grassroots. Most were professional ecologists or science teachers. All were short on finances but long on volunteer spirit, giving hours of their time to write newsletters, organize outings, and dream A Rocha dreams. When Karin and Alain Boisclair-Joly returned from serving with A Rocha in Lebanon they joined the Board, and soon after Karin was employed as A Rocha's first Canadian staff—for a whopping ten hours per week. Squirreled away in a tiny office under a staircase, she was A Rocha's administrative point person for getting the creation care word out to the wider Christian community.

Our first challenge in this regard was to establish A Rocha as a legitimate Christian ministry. The subtext of our name back then, *Christians in Conservation*, read like an oxymoron to many whose only category for environmentalists was of hippie types with strong body odor and a penchant for chaining themselves to trees they'd named "Egeria." We ran into such typecasting when we inquired about setting up a booth at a large Christian conference in the area. We actually were not asking whether we *could* set up a booth, but *how much* it would cost. We were truly shocked, therefore, when we were informed that we were not welcome because our work was not deemed Christian mission. Ten years later our staff have led workshops and seminars at this same conference, which just goes to show how far attitudes have changed. It seems tree hugging and Christianity have something in common after all.

STEPPING FORWARD

Karin's work was invaluable in getting A Rocha off the ground, but it quickly became clear that full-time staff were needed if we were to see significant conservation and education programs established. And so the Board drew straws. Sort of. One September evening the eight or so members of the Board sat in a circle and took turns saying whether or not they'd be willing to be the first director of this vulnerable little thing. The caveat, of course, was that there was no salary, a minor detail that no one thought would hinder the employment process. In the end it wasn't so much that Markku and I put ourselves forward, but that everyone else stepped back, leaving us standing alone and eager on the starting line.

When it came time to break the news to our parents—that Markku was going to leave his well-paying job as an Environmental Consultant, which meant leaving his twelfth-floor downtown office with a view of the Vancouver Yacht Club for a desk in our basement—we framed the vocational shift in a flattering light. We might have even hinted at something like crème de la crème entrepreneurial directors needed for this exciting new initiative. In reality the hiring process was more like a pot put on to boil; rather than the crème ladled from the top, we were the lonely little potatoes left over at the bottom.

At any rate, we realized immediately where our gifts lay—in vision and enthusiasm, but definitely not in administration and the nuts and bolts of what it takes to get a non-profit off the ground (exciting stuff like database systems and donor receipting). It was thus with great delight that we welcomed the incredibly competent Patrick Lilley to join us. His hard work and amazing ability to do just about anything—from rattling off the Latin names of plants to resurrecting a malfunctioning computer system—quickly made him an invaluable member of our three-person A Rocha team. Since Karin's closet was no longer available and none of our cupboards fit both Markku and Patrick, the office moved to our home's basement and then to the basement of St. Clement's Anglican Church down the road in Lynn Valley, North Vancouver.

ENCOUNTERING INUITS

Those early days were heady, but also stressful. The primary stress lay in the fundraising and time required to get A Rocha out of the nest and into the air. In hindsight I'm amazed at the blasé attitude with which we initially approached both these hurdles. Markku left his job on a Friday in early March and started with A Rocha the following Monday. He'd been working full-steam for an environmental consulting firm and I was busy figuring out how to be a new mom, so we hadn't given much attention to fundraising for our salary. In fact, the only thing we did was send out a single letter stating our needs and then hoped and prayed for the best. The best proved to be a number of commitments of financial support, the biggest coming from our church, Capilano Christian Community, which staggered us with a start-up commitment that came to one-sixth of our goal. After a couple of months we were about halfway to our goal (which we randomly chose as a beginning teacher's salary in B.C.). Of course, half a salary wouldn't support us, so Markku spent many of his evenings plugging away at environmental consulting contracts, which helped cover the personal bills. But there was still a lot of money to raise, not only for our salary, but for the general budget, which included a portion of Patrick's salary and general operating expenses.

Needless to say, the combination of long work hours and the lack of funds was stressful! I remember one particularly bleak

afternoon in late spring when things came to a breaking point. The
A Rocha honeymoon was over and sheer vision was not going to
carry us any further. Markku and I sat despondently on our bed
while baby Maya entertained herself in a pile of rumpled laundry.
I was mad at Markku for leaving his secure, well paying job and
Markku was mad at me for hatching up the whole A Rocha idea
in the first place. Curt words were exchanged, tears were shed, and
despair set in. We were ready to quit. We needed a sign. Now, we
are not normally sign and wonders kind of Christians, but even an
atheist prays for a miracle in the foxhole, and this was our foxhole.

In this regard, I am reminded of that old man-walks-into-a-
bar story:

> "I'm done with religion," a man tells the proverbial bar-
> tender. "I was up in Alaska, see. Stranded on this ice drift.
> And I pray to God to rescue me."
>
> "So?" says the bartender.
>
> "So, two days pass and nothing happens. Finally, just
> when I'm thinking I'm going to die, along comes these
> Eskimos."
>
> "And?" says the bartender.
>
> "And they pick me up in their boat and rescue me."
>
> "So God came through in the end." says the bartender,
> satisfied.
>
> "What?" says the man. "It was the Eskimos that rescued
> me while God sat on his hands."

Our story had a couple of Inuits in it too. As I said, we were in a pit,
completely daunted by the task of launching A Rocha in Canada
and in particular of raising the funds to see it through. And so we
prayed (after a good bit of sulking). We prayed specifically that
God would send us someone older and wiser to encourage us and
pray with us. We decided not to call anyone, but to wait and see
who would turn up. We went for a walk at the beach. We picked
the busiest beach on Vancouver's North Shore (we'd prayed for a
miracle, but we weren't against upping the odds of running into
someone we knew). With each step we glanced about, expecting a
familiar and godly face to beam out at us from the crowd.

But not one did. We walked for over two miles along the West Vancouver Seawall in total anonymity and then drove home in silence. The day passed. No one showed. God, it seemed, was sitting on his hands while we huddled, shivering on our iceberg, adrift.

But then—dum, dum dum!—early the next day Uncle Tarmo knocked on our door. Now you have to understand that Markku's Uncle Tarmo had never just shown up before. Never in the thirteen years that we've been married has he just dropped in unannounced. Furthermore, though his name conjures images of someone furry, possibly blue, and Muppetish, he very much fit the "older and wiser" bill. His visit was full of encouraging stories of firsthand accounts of God's provision during his days as a Bible smuggler in the former Soviet Union. (I'm not making this up— he really was a Bible smuggler in Russia.) At the end of his visit he asked if he could pray for us. He prayed specifically that God would *confirm* his calling to us and provide for the needs of this fledgling ministry. And then he left.

The very next day we got a letter and a sizable donation in the mail, thus ending the donation drought. The financial gift was tremendously encouraging, but it was the letter—the only letter to accompany any donation to that point—that really staggered us. In the letter our older and wiser friend Irene wrote (and I quote), "Your qualifications would *confirm* that you are the couple to fulfill the task ahead. May God's Holy Spirit guide, support, direct and comfort you in the days ahead."

Hmmm.

The writer Anne Lamott comments on such events when she writes, "The nonreligious types think, 'Well, that's a funny little coincidence,' but we Holy Rollers say that coincidence is just God working anonymously."

So, we persevered.

SETTING UP SHOP

We knew that our home of North Vancouver would probably not be the long-term base for A Rocha's work in B.C. Our goal was to set up a Field Study Center like the one established in Portugal by Peter and Miranda twenty years earlier. To do this we wanted to be in an area that would benefit from our presence. We were hoping for a place with environmentally sensitive habitat that needed protecting, but which didn't have a host of people already trying to protect it. Markku's job on A Rocha's Board had been to investigate possible conservation areas, and we had spent many a weekend tooling around the Lower Mainland of B.C., exploring possible sites. We kept this up for our first two years on staff until we stumbled upon Boundary Bay and the Little Campbell Watershed.

Actually, at this point in the story I am boldly going to take credit for landing A Rocha in the Little Campbell Watershed. But lest anyone think I had some clairvoyant insight into its ecological worth and suitability, let me hasten to add that I zeroed in on this bit of geography for purely selfish reasons. You see, my twin sister was then living in Washington state about an hour south of the Canadian border, and it struck me that if A Rocha's Center were positioned as southerly as possible, cross border rendezvouses would be happily convenient.

So, finger on the map, I casually asked Markku, "What about this bit down by the border? It has this big bay and some interesting looking rivers."

Markku pondered and we began reconnaissance missions to check out the area. The more we poked around, the more it seemed that Boundary Bay made sense. Not only did the area comprise one of Canada's most significant Important Bird Areas, it was also home to the Little Campbell Watershed, which drained intact, via a beautiful estuary, into the Pacific Ocean. Finally, in comparison to other environmentally sensitive areas in B.C.'s Lower Mainland, surprisingly few people were working to preserve it.

Markku met with municipal leaders as well the director of Friends of Semiahmoo Bay, the most active local stewardship group, led by the indomitable Marg Cuthbert. They all gave us an enthusiastic invitation to set up shop in the watershed. Markku joined a couple of local conservation groups and after monthly meetings would drive the back roads of South Surrey looking for potential properties that might serve as an environmental center.

Lo and behold, he came home late one night from the Little Campbell Watershed Society all in a dither about a fabulous property quaintly called "Heritage Acres." He wondered if we could drive back down the next day to see it. I looked down at my belly and wondered if he were mad. I was two weeks shy of my due date with our second child and I wasn't going anywhere, thank you very much. Markku relented and paced the house, waiting for baby Bryn to be born.

One month later a two-week old Bryn paid her first visit to the future A Rocha Environmental Center. With two ponds, pasture land, a small cedar forest, a tree house, log cabin, outdoor washrooms, two houses, and a heritage barn—all packed into ten tidy acres—the place put us in mind more of A Rocha Disney than the humble A Rocha Center we had visited in Portugal. The only thing it lacked was a roller coaster! Lest we lose perspective in light of all the property's perks, we were aided in our evaluation by a list of eight criteria the Board had prescribed for the future center property, among them: two dwellings for staff and interns, proximity to transit, a variety of habitats and proximity to the Little Campbell River. Check, check, check. Heritage Acres fit the bill in every category.

That first visit was rather comical, thanks to the sellers' real estate agent, who didn't get us at all. He'd heard that we wanted to start a Field *Study* Center and so on the initial tour, he would pause at picturesque spots overlooking the pond or in the woods and say, "Now, this would be a lovely spot for your people to *study*." And then a few moments later, at another beautiful location, "Ah, here's another perfect spot where your people could *study*." I think he thought we were starting a giant outdoor study hall.

But the owners, Harriet and Irwin Leitz, "got" us. So we sidestepped the real estate agents (though they still got their commissions in the end!) and asked for a personal meeting. The defining moment came when we sat down in the barn with the Leitzes.

"So," said Harriet. "How serious are you about this property?"

"Quite serious," said Markku.

Pause.

"But," he went on, clearing his throat and furrowing his brow in a sincere knot. "I have to be honest, A Rocha doesn't have a penny in the bank."

Pause.

"Well," said Harriet, her words weighted for emphasis. "I'm sure you've been praying about it as we have."

It was an "Aha" moment that opened the door for a joint journey of faith for both A Rocha and the Leitzes. We all learned to be open handed as we entered a three-month long dialogue regarding price and terms. A few times the purchase seemed truly dead in the water, but finally a deal was struck, which included both a significant gift from the Leitzes and also a remarkably generous arrangement whereby they'd carry the mortgage, the first year interest free. Of course, not having an aforementioned penny in the bank meant that A Rocha had no money for a down payment and so Harriet and Irwin, in a continued show of generosity and faith, agreed to an experiment. They would stay living on site in their home and the Kostamos would move into the old farmhouse across the lawn. We would have four months to come up with $250,000. If we didn't, the deal was off—we'd move out and A Rocha would wait for something else.

COUNTDOWN

A few days into that first month I asked Markku, "So, what exactly is your plan for raising all this money?" I'm well aware that this makes me sound like a chump. It makes me sound like Ma Ingalls in her most simpering simplicity, ready to be dragged hither and yon at the whim of a restless husband. Actually, I probably was a bit of a chump. I was also tremendously sleep-deprived, what with juggling two kids under three and welcoming a constant stream of volunteers and visitors—who started arriving almost moments after we did. I frankly didn't have the energy to strategize how we were going to raise all that money.

Markku, however, did have a plan and it centered on a little inner-city church in East Vancouver. The members of Grandview Calvary Baptist, home church of our Board Chair, stunned us with their generosity. An elderly member had left the church a very large donation, which was slated for a low-income housing project. Since that project was still a couple years off, we boldly asked for a loan—for the entire amount of the down payment. The church called a meeting and voted. To give us half. Interest free. It was an amazing act of solidarity and grace.

It also provided a profound lesson in fundraising: don't put all your eggs in one basket. While their offer was magnanimous in the extreme—given we were a bit of a high risk venture, never mind the fact that we weren't even Baptist—we had naively been hoping to be loaned the entire amount. But in their wisdom, the members of Grandview Calvary understood that, in the long run, a sugar daddy can be a crippling benefactor for a non-profit.

And so with six weeks to the down payment deadline we were scrambling to come up with another $125,000. We wracked our brains for someone to ask. Bono seemed distracted by Africa. Gates had the malaria thing tying up his thoughts and finances. Oprah had her own gig with a girls' school in South Africa. Who to call? When we lowered our sights to our own friends and relations they all seemed too humbly situated to be able to swing such a big gift or loan.

Just as things began to look bleak Markku had a conversation with a not so rich, but very well connected friend in Vancouver. It went something like this:

Friend: "You know the thing I like about you, Markku?"

Markku: (In an *ah shucks* kind of way) "What's that?"

Friend: "You're so needy."

Markku: "Ah, shucks."

Taking this conversation as an invitation to display yet more neediness, Markku asked him to set up a meeting with the most sympathetic philanthropist he knew. That person turned out to be Ken Smith, who gladly agreed to visit the property with his wife the following week.

"It's like the promised land!" Ken exclaimed, picking an apple from a tree in the orchard. We were just finishing a tour of the property and heading inside for tea. Ken and his wife, Ruth, were enamored by the site and the vision of a Christian environmental center dedicated to conservation and education. They had read Peter Harris' book, *Under the Bright Wings*, which tells the story of A Rocha's first project in Portugal, as a warm-up to the visit and were encouraged to find that they resonated thoroughly with A Rocha's approach to mission.

Despite all this going for us, we sat fidgeting at the kitchen table, chatting about everything under the sun except money. We were new to the fundraising game and had no idea how to ask someone for so much cash. So, we didn't. Thankfully Ken was a seasoned philanthropist and, seeing our inability to grasp the nettle, he leaned across the table, looked into our eyes and said, "What can I do for you?"

And we made the down payment deadline.

EIGHT YEARS LATER

Now here's the funny thing. While we did raise a fair chunk of change, we were never able to raise the whole amount. Not even close. We did eventually pay out the Leitzes, but we did so through a bond offering that served as a second mortgage, complete with interest. Over the years, carrying this debt, we questioned whether A Rocha had been rash to jump into property ownership so quickly. Perhaps we should have bided our time—waited for a windfall so we could buy a site outright. Who knows?

We do know this: That first Center allowed A Rocha to welcome thousands of visitors, as well as hundreds of interns, day campers, and school kids. That Center allowed us to grow literally tons of organic vegetables, serve thousands of meals, and conduct conservation research on a myriad of species. That first Center allowed us to do all these things with a measure of intentionality as we strove to be true to our convictions regarding creation care, hospitality, and justice.

3

Subterranean Grace
in a World of Wounds

I believe in my heart that faith in Jesus Christ can and will lead us beyond an exclusive concern for the well-being of other human beings to the broader concern for the well-being of the birds in our backyard, the fish in our rivers, and every living creature on the face of the earth.

John Wesley

It sounds like a bad joke: what do you get when a Buddhist, a Christian, and a Wiccan sit down for a meal together? Actually, it was one Buddhist, three Christians, one Wiccan, and three agnostics and what you got was some amazing conversation. This montage of folks came to A Rocha as part of a University of British Columbia Earth Sciences class that required participation in a community service project. They had chosen the topic "religion and the environment," which made A Rocha a perfect fit. After spending five days at our Center renovating a musty quonset hut into a glorified dorm room, we sat down to a big dinner to thank them for their hard work.

Candles were lit, the table was spread, and we sat to the feast. The conversation was lively and centered on beliefs. We didn't have an agenda in this regard, we simply asked these students to share a bit of their own stories and, being thoughtful university students, they zeroed in on what motivated them to care about the earth. They shared their genuine grappling with issues of sustainability, the plight of the poor, and their own struggles with the Christian faith in these regards. We sat for hours. I felt tempted to look over my shoulder to see if there were cameras rolling somewhere. In my family of origin, dinner parties were a stage for storytelling and raucous laughter, not profound musings on the mysterious workings of the universe, and I felt like I was in a well-scripted foreign film.

Soon they were directing their questions toward us. What motivated us? What did we believe? One asked how our Christian faith informed our work in conservation. Another commented on how he saw those working in the environmental field struggle with despair and wondered where we found hope. Lastly, sweet Lo—an agnostic girl with a church background—asked what did we think was the purpose behind humanity's existence. You know, simple questions. The amazing thing was the openness with which these questions were asked, as if they really expected to find some granule of truth in our response.

While not claiming to have all the answers, we shared a bit of our own stories and how we'd personally found hope and purpose. Markku's journey through divorce and the depression that accompanied it added authenticity to his narrative. Hard not to be on the side of someone who has survived some rough knocks. Eyes moistened in sympathy as Markku spoke of lying on a big boulder in the middle of Lynn Creek and tangibly sensing God's love for him when—especially when—the rest of his life was falling apart.

The apex of the conversation came in response to the "What gives you hope?" question. We responded by considering how the incarnation shows God's commitment to creation—the Creator becomes the created in the ultimate act of solidarity. Ian, the Buddhist, and Christa, the Wiccan, seemed utterly stunned by this idea. Christianity suddenly was no longer an unattractive code of ethics but a divine adventure of reckless love. Christa said she'd be up all night, her mind whirling with the implications. Ian said believing this would make all the difference in how one treated the world.

Touché.

Belief matters. We work in conservation because we believe certain things about God and the world. Following is a quick sketch of a few of the beliefs that inform our work.

1. THE EARTH IS THE LORD'S

Early on A Rocha took on Psalm 24:1 as its inspiration: "The Earth is the Lord's and everything in it." Though seemingly benign in its simplicity the proposition that the earth actually belongs to God and not us is radical and often runs counter to popular Christian beliefs. Allow me to illustrate.

I was visiting a church recently where an enthusiastic man in a plaid tie presented a PowerPoint of images taken from the Hubble telescope. His presentation—set to a soundtrack full of wavering strings and fluttering flutes—showed swirling galaxies, frosty nebulas, and myriads of sparkling stars. The presenter said he was "blown away" that God had created all this—the whole universe!—just for him. Indeed, all of creation was a present, gift-wrapped in starry paper, for God's beloved: humankind. I looked around the room expecting to see mouths agape—some sign of this man's mistaken conclusion. But no, everyone wore those cheery smiles, so appropriate for modest Christian folk.

I'm not sure where we got the idea that creation is the possession of people, but it sure isn't the message of the Bible. True, the creation narrative in Genesis does set humans in a unique position among the rest of creation—though, as Barbara Brown

Taylor points out, we don't even get our own day, but must share Day Six with all manner of creeping things, including *cows*! The specialness bestowed on our species, Genesis says, has to do with our being "created in the image of God." We reflect God's character uniquely which, rather than giving us divine-size egos, should humble us to no end and clue us in to the fact that we might have a special role to play in the grand drama of creation.

The notion that we are image-bearers coupled with the idea that the earth belongs to God has major implications for how we live and how we respond to God's charge to Adam to "serve the garden and keep it" (Gen 2:15). Cal DeWitt, professor of environmental studies at the University of Wisconsin-Madison, helpfully sheds light on this verse when he unpacks the Hebrew words for serve (*abad*) and keep (*shamar*). The first, *abad*, is sometimes translated *till*, *dress*, or *work*—all good gardening words, but it is the second word, *shamar*, that puts a new spin on what it means to be a good gardener for God. *Shamar* is sometimes translated *tend*, *guard*, *take care of*, and *look after*. DeWitt contends that *shamar* implies a "loving, caring, sustaining type of keeping." The word is the same used in the Aaronic blessing: "The Lord bless you and *keep* you; the Lord make his face shine upon you and give you peace" (Num 6:24–25). Dewitt writes:

> When we invoke God's blessing to keep us, we are not asking that God keep us in a kind of preserved, inactive, uninteresting state. Instead we are calling on God to keep us in all of our vitality, with all of our energy and beauty. The keeping we expect of God when we invoke the Aaronic blessing is one that nurtures all of our life-sustaining and life-fulfilling relationships with our family members, with our neighbors and our friends, with the land, air, and water, and with our God. We ask God to love us, to care for us, and to sustain us in relationship to our natural and human environment . . . The rich and full keeping that we invoke with the Aaronic blessing is the kind of rich and full keeping that we should bring to God's garden, to God's creatures, and to all of creation.

All this points to our special role in creation, which is one of care-taking or stewarding. In fact, it is our unique position as image-bearers that qualifies us to steward God's creation. "Made in the divine image, we are here to love as God loves," writes Barbara Brown Taylor. "You know how it feels under the shadow of those wings? So move over. Make room, because there is a whole creation seeking refuge, and you, you are the spitting image of the One who gives life to all."

Finally, as a kind of sidebar on worship: if the Earth is the Lord's, then it's appropriate to acknowledge this once in a while. I love what Taylor has to say on this point: "For those of us who believe God is the source from which all arose, we are the first creatures to say so out loud. God may well prefer the sound of spring peepers, but I have to believe there was joy in heaven when the first human being looked at the sky and said, 'Thank you for all of this.'"

2. CREATION IS GOOD

"God saw everything that he had made, and indeed, it was very good" (Gen 1:31).

My mother-in law wears a bikini. She is seventy years old and decades of gravity have done their work. But she wears a bikini nonetheless, with a devil-may-care nonchalance to what others her age are more inclined to cover in sarongs, ruffles, and cruise-wear.

She's my hero.

Her okay-ness with her body has a twofold source. First, she's Finnish. Do you know any Finns? Untouched by the Puritan prudishness that is historically English and North American, they share a continental European lack of modesty concerning the body, but to the extreme. While other Europeans are going topless on the warm and sunny beaches of the French Rivera, the Finns are flinging themselves buck naked from their saunas into the *snow*. There's a reason to take off your shirt in the south of France—it's hot! But why subject your private parts to the crunch and scrape of ice in the dead of winter? I don't have answer, even though I live with a

Finn who regularly goes in for the naked sauna/snow frolicking thing. But, the point is, Finns are profoundly okay with their bodies.

SWIMWEAR OF CHOICE

EXHIBIT A:

my mother-in-law's
age: seventy
nationality: Finnish

How does this relate to Christian theology? My mother-in-law is also a devout Christian and I think her embrace of the bikini as her swimwear of choice goes beyond her Finnish heritage to her biblical understanding of creation. She understands that when it says in the Bible that Adam was formed out of the dirt (*adama* in Hebrew) that she too is a *human* formed out of *humus* and that humus is good. She actually believes that when it says, "God saw all that he had made and it was good," that means her body as well. It also means mountains and trees and iguanas, but one's body is a great place to start.

Theologically, the idea that the material world is good makes sense—after all, God wouldn't have taken on a human body himself if flesh were inherently evil. Christians believe Jesus was fully God *and* fully man. Yes, he came to redeem the world, but he did so eating and drinking, walking, and sleeping. And working. Jesus was a carpenter, for goodness sake—he worked with wood, with callused hands and with sweat in his eyes.

If matter is good and Jesus fully "materialized"—that is, he participated fully in the material life that all humans participate in—then that puts an end to silly Gnostic and dualistic notions of a material/spiritual divide. It certainly sheds a holy light on woodworking! It also sheds a holy light on all manner of "earthy" jobs, from ditch digging to diaper changing to gardening to fish and frog studying.

If the material/spiritual divide is only an intellectual construct, then how does one do one's work Christianly? Does the Christian biologist hum hymns while checking amphibian cover boards for signs of salamanders? Does she exclaim, "Praise the Lord!" when measuring a fresh water mussel, discovering it's over one hundred years old? Does she preach to the birds as St. Francis was said to have done? Maybe. But more fundamentally, she approaches her vocation and her tasks with a degree of reverence that acknowledges the goodness of creation and the creator who made it.

3. EVERYTHING IS CONNECTED

I realize this is one of the primary themes of this whole book, but in this case I am not referring to food chains or webs of life, but moral choices and the related webs of relationship that flow from them. While the first two beliefs center on the goodness of creation, the third turns on the idea that humankind's broken relationship with God leads to a broken relationship with other people and with creation itself. Consider the words of Hosea 4:1–3:

> Hear the word of the LORD, you Israelites,
> because the LORD has a charge to bring
> against you who live in the land:
> "There is no faithfulness, no love,
> no acknowledgment of God in the land.
> There is only cursing, lying and murder,
> stealing and adultery;
> they break all bounds,
> and bloodshed follows bloodshed.
> Because of this the land mourns,
> and all who live in it waste away;
> the beasts of the field and the birds of the air
> and the fish of the sea are dying."

Cheery passage. Although it was written thousands of years ago, these words sound startlingly similar to many newspaper headlines today. Fish, birds, and beasts die. Murder, theft, and adultery abound. People have lost their faith in God. Sounds like the *New*

York Times to me. But whereas the *New York Times* presents such a cattle call of calamities in stand-alone articles, Hosea connects them, showing the ripple effect of sin. Creation's suffering is intrinsically linked to humanity's faithlessness, lack of love, and lack of acknowledgment of God. The trickle-down effect of our brokenness is a land that mourns and all (humans and non-humans) who live in it waste away. This is certainly what we are seeing around the world today. The UN recently reported that environmental refugees (people who are displaced because of environmental degradation) already outnumber refugees as a result of conflict. Conflicts will, in fact, be increasingly driven by the scarcity of natural resources (read: a mourning land).

It is no surprise that most major relief and community development organizations are beginning to figure "the environment" into their programs. World Vision's *Child View Magazine*, for example, has a "Green Page" with tips on how we in the industrialized West can change our over-consumptive lifestyles for the benefit of those in the more impoverished regions on the world. Peter Harris recently told me that A Rocha International gets, on average, a request a week from various nonprofits asking for help in applying environmental solutions to their poverty relief work.

I know what you're thinking: Hold on—isn't it precisely those who believe in God who often do the most damage to the environment? Isn't it the industrialized West, which is full of Christians, that is raping and pillaging the earth for their citizens' own gain, leaving the fish, birds, and innocent humans to suffer in impoverished landscapes? Well, yes.

So, allow me to qualify my remarks. I don't think simply believing in God is enough. What is needed, and what Hosea says the people of his day were lacking, is love. Love, rooted in faith, gives us the humility to see our greed for what it is and what it causes— suffering for the Earth and its inhabitants. Love, not idealized or sentimental, but practical and concrete, gives us the courage to make the connection.

4. WE ARE TO HAVE HOPE

Hope is a rare commodity in the environmental world, as our University of British Columbia friends pointed out. One of the liabilities of an ecological education, writes Aldo Leopold, is that one "lives alone in a world of wounds." Knowing what conservationists know, it's only logical that they would be tempted to despair. But the Christian way is one of hope. Consider Paul's words in Colossians (1:15–20):

> He [Jesus] is the image of the invisible God, the firstborn over all creation. For by him all things were created: things in heaven and on earth, visible and invisible, whether thrones or powers or rulers or authorities; all things were created by him and for him. He is before all things, and in him all things hold together. And he is the head of the body, the church; he is the beginning and the firstborn from among the dead, so that in everything he might have the supremacy. For God was pleased to have all his fullness dwell in him, and through him to reconcile to himself all things, whether things on earth or things in heaven, by making peace through his blood, shed on the cross.

This is a passage that roots us in hope—hope that some day, somehow, some way redemption is possible for all things. In this passage Paul links creation and humanity's redemption through the person of Jesus. Through Christ *all things* were created; he sustains *all things* (holds them together), and then through his resurrection he reconciles *all things*. Where might *all things* stop, do you think? Does it stop with people? That is how I used to read it. But the radical point this passage seems to be making is that creation itself participates in redemption. It is our anthropocentric view of the world that causes us to read *all things* as *all people*.

Paul hits on this theme of creation's redemption in the book of Romans as well when he speaks of creation "waiting . . . in hope that it will be set free from its bondage to decay and will obtain the freedom of the glory of the children of God" (8:20–21). New Testament scholar Gordon Fee explains that Paul is not setting out an argument for creation's redemption; rather, he takes it as a given.

Creation's redemption is part of the warp and woof of his first-century Jewish worldview, and he includes it here in a way that assumes his readers already believe it as well. He uses creation's groaning and hoping for release as a metaphor for our own suffering and our own eventual redemption. Creation's "hope" in a future redemption is meant to bulwark our own human hope in the midst of trials.

There are all sorts of rabbit trails we could follow at this point. Will my cat Jeffrey be in heaven? What about pelicans and pine trees? And how about mosquitoes? I have no idea and no inclination to follow such a trail (in writing, at least). Paul and the rest of the New Testament writers never spell out in any satisfying detail what creation's redemption will look like practically. This is not their primary concern. Their primary concern is the overarching theme of redemption for all of creation, which is meant to root us in hope—a hope centered on God's ultimate care for what he has made. This hope allows us to "be joyful though we have considered all the facts," as Wendell Berry says. Hope, if it's true, runs deep, with taproots nourished by a subterranean grace that flows strong and swift despite outer circumstances. It is what keeps us going.

SUMMING UP

That's an overview in very broad brushstrokes of a few of the things I believe. I am well aware of the obvious problem of proof-texting, which lends itself so easily to the twisting of scripture to prove all sorts of crazy positions—from polygamy to misogyny to stupidity. I chose the scripture verses I did, not because they are the only ones that deal with creation, but because they touch on themes that run throughout scripture—themes of creation and steward-ship and justice and non-duality. Am I picking and choosing? Perhaps. Is this all I believe? Certainly not.

Finally, just because I believe that creation care *is* Christian work does not mean I believe that the task of earthkeeping is the *only*, or even the most important, work a Christian should be do-ing. Because I've taken ecology's pattern of interconnectedness seriously I understand that the gospel functions in much the same way. Biblically understood, the church is one body made up of many parts, and it takes all parts to live out a whole gospel. There-fore, I applaud the caring community development worker, the humble evangelist, the erudite theologian, the dogged relief work-er, the clever novelist, and the compassionate civil rights activist. All these are potential messengers of God's love and help bring God's kingdom to earth. I just don't think one is better or more important than the others—we need them all (just like we need construction workers, police officers, parents and artists who see their vocations as "spiritual" callings). But let's not be reductionis-tic here. While creation care as *a vocation* is a specific calling, as *a way of life* it is everyone's calling. Just as every Christian is called to witness to God's love and to promote justice for those without a voice, so too, all Christians are called to steward creation.

4

A Family of Cracked Pots

Inclusion is the first step toward transformation.

DEANA STROM

MARKKU AND I HAD just laid out an array of brochures, books, and newsletters on an information table at the back of a church one Sunday morning when an elderly woman tottered up, eyes fixed on our A Rocha banner. Expecting an ally, we gave her wide, sincere smiles and waited for her to declare her abiding interest in birds, bugs, or anything biological. Instead she studied our banner a few pregnant seconds more.

Then, hungrily, she asked, "Are you folks with that candy company?"

We drew a blank.

"Candy company?" we queried.

"Al-mond Ro-cha?" she said slowly as if we were a bit dim-witted.

"Ah! Oh. Well, no." We apologized that we had no goodies to give her and tried to explain that we were a Christian conservation organization.

She drew a blank.

"We take care of cre-a-tion," we said slowly as if *she* were a bit dim-witted.

A tiny light of understanding dawned in her eyes. "Well, you have a weird name," she said and shuffled off toward the sanctuary.

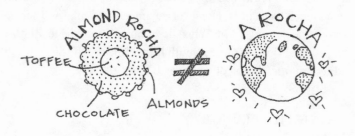

WHAT'S IN A NAME?

Indeed, "A Rocha" is an odd handle for a conservation organization, particularly in North America, where it starts people salivating and dreaming of chocolate covered toffees. First there's the question of pronunciation. (It's *a-raw-sha* for the uninitiated.) Then there's the question of meaning. (It means "the rock" in Portuguese because the first Environmental Center was located at Quinta da A Rocha—"Farm on the Rock.") In spite of the awkwardness of the name we deliberately chose to stick with it because it connotes the Latin flavor and core commitments of the organization. No, we don't all lie down for a communal nap at two in the afternoon. But we do eat a lot of meals together, all of which tend to be spacious in their time boundaries. Why? Because meal times are fodder for relationships, and relationships are at the core of what we do. All of A Rocha's activities, in fact, are grounded in community, giving our work impetus and meaning.

Having learned the lesson of ecology well, we realize that no living thing exists in isolation. It's obvious that in biological terms it is impossible to be truly independent, else, what would one eat, breathe, or drink? The stronger the biological interconnections, the stronger the creature. Likewise sociologically, we are interconnected through webs of relationships that, when strong, translate into emotional and spiritual health and well-being. Therefore, we are committed to caring for *all* of God's creation in holistic ways— the more threatened zoological bits, but also the more threatened human bits too. We chose to do this by modeling our Environmental Center after A Rocha's first center in Portugal, which has functioned much like a guest house for volunteers and interns desiring to study the natural world. When describing this model to others I often suggest they imagine a youth hostel "meets" the Sierra Club and set the whole thing on an organic farm.

TAKING THE PLUNGE

Our Center in Surrey has room to host up to ten interns and volunteers. Those who come conduct wildlife surveys, help with habitat enhancement of salmon streams, educate children in day camps, and get their hands very dirty growing vegetables in our Community Shared Agriculture Project. Some local students get paid through an annual government grant, but most do all this work without remuneration. You'd think we'd have a hard time finding folks to do all this for free, but we set out our shingle and they came—from all over the world, in fact. Over the past eight years, our interns and volunteers have hailed from Brazil, Cambodia, Canada, China, Colombia, England, France, Germany, Holland, Indonesia, Ireland, Israel, Malaysia, Saudi Arabia, Singapore, Scotland, South Africa, and the USA. Of course, they come from near and far not just to work for free, but to be trained, to pad their resumés or to have an adventure far from home. Whatever their reasons, almost all are drawn to the fact that they get to do these things with others who will dig, study, and play with them.

We jumped right into the deep end of community living when we moved to the Center. While the deal to purchase the property was still in the works, inquiries about visiting or volunteering were already being lobbed at us and, being hopeful types, Markku and I said yes to them all. Thus it happened that we moved into the property's old farmhouse on August 1st and the first volunteer arrived August 3rd, which left us one whole day to unpack. Actually, the fact that we got any unpacking done at all was because our first volunteer *did* arrive two days after us. She was a godsend. Her name was Carolyn and she came from Germany. She spoke perfect English and was unwaveringly cheerful, but with a quiet demeanor—your perfect volunteer. Most volunteers and interns come to do something specific like conservation, education, or farming—Carolyn came to be helpful. And so I made her my personal servant and Maya's personal playmate. She spent hours playing with Maya on the lawn outside our kitchen window while I wore baby Bryn on my back and scurried about unpacking boxes, making meals (for the other, not quite so helpful, visitors), and writing thank you letters to those who were writing a steady stream of donation checks in response to Markku's fundraising efforts. Carolyn and Maya formed a fast friendship, evidenced when Carolyn left two months later as she knelt by my daughter, held both her small hands in her own, and wept.

In light of this first visitor experience I find it interesting that before we dove into community living, I wasted a great deal of time worrying. Mainly I worried about our children's safety. *What if someone molests them?* was worry number one. *What if they get exposed to too much too soon?* came close on its heels. Don't get me wrong, we haven't become blasé about our kids' well being. We are still moderately vigilant. Nevertheless, living in community inevitably opens possibilities for younger members to be introduced to "learning" beyond their years. Like, for example, when six-year-old Bryn helped an intern fold her laundry and discovered all sorts of things about female intimate apparel. Afterwards she searched me out to ask why anyone would prefer a string instead of a nice swath of fabric to cover one's behind. Still, in hindsight (no pun intended),

I'm intrigued that before actually embarking on community living I thought more about the potential dangers than the benefits.

WELCOMING THE STRANGER

Could it be that I focused more on the hazards than the benefits of community living because I was raised in a society of *Stranger Danger*, where anyone not commended as a friend, or at least a friend of a friend, is a potential bogeyman? In light of our societal obsession with protection and security it is interesting that, as Barbara Brown Taylor points out, the biblical tradition of encountering a stranger is that of hospitality. In fact, the Greek word for hospitality—*philoxenia*—assumes a reaching out to those unknown. Taken apart, the word literally means love of stranger: *philo*, for love, and *xenia*, for stranger. The Hebrew take on hospitality is just as outward looking as the Greek. Jonathan Sacks, Great Britain's chief rabbi, writes, "The Hebrew Bible in one verse commands, 'You shall love your neighbor as yourself,' but in no fewer than 36 places commands us to 'love the stranger.'" Jesus joins the two in the parable of the Good Samaritan, explaining that the stranger is really and truly also one's own neighbor.

Of course to really encounter a stranger you have to be able to make eye contact. Contact with the Holy Spirit is also helpful. Tiina Hildebrant had both these bases covered. Tiina served as A Rocha's office manager for about four years. She had an ear tuned to God's whisper and eyes ready to make contact with whomever crossed her path, as the following story illustrates.

One evening Tiina was traveling back from Vancouver to the A Rocha Center by public transport. She had boarded the Skytrain, which would zip her down to Surrey and her A Rocha home, when she felt the tug of God's Spirit telling her get off and take the 351 bus instead (which involved some significant backtracking into the heart of downtown late at night). Most of us might have interpreted such a tug as mere fantasy. But Tiina both heard and heeded what she assumed was God's delightful opportunity for her in that particular moment.

So she retraced her steps downtown, got lost for a few bewildering moments when she emerged from the Skytrain station, met a woman going in the right direction, and finally found the 351 bus stop. There she encountered a young and friendly looking Arab man. She made eye contact. They struck up a conversation. It turns out Ali was a student from the Middle East and was staying with his former English teacher in Surrey just three kilometers from our Center. They boarded the bus and took a seat together. They chatted about their families, life in Canada, the usual small talk. With about twenty minutes left in the trip Ali asked if Tiina knew where he might be able to volunteer during his six-week visit. He wanted to practice his English and be of use, he explained. She told him she worked for a Christian environmental organization and that we were always on the lookout for volunteers. When she learned he had a knack with computers she asked if he would like to help with some of our IT needs.

On his first visit he seemed unduly excited. He explained that when he'd told his host family about meeting Tiina and about this group called A Rocha they were flabbergasted. Turns out they knew all about A Rocha since they had visited the A Rocha Center in France and were very keen on the organization. They had no idea, however, that A Rocha had a center in Canada, let alone one just a few kilometers from their house! Ironically, they might have been some of the only people living in the city of Surrey at that time who had any inkling of what A Rocha was, even if they had no inkling that we existed nearby.

Ali came twice a week for about a month. He ate meals, tinkered with computers, and made friends with everyone. Over lunch hour and during breaks he battered us with questions about the environment, Christian faith, Canadian culture. He showed us pictures of the sports cars he and his friends raced in the desert on weekends. He told us he couldn't show us a picture of his fiancee because the Muslim code of ethics did not permit women's faces to be photographed. He was fascinated by Christianity. Someone gave him a Bible. Before he left he cooked everyone a Saudi Arabian feast in appreciation of his time with us. A few years later, he visited with his new wife, returning to us like the true friend he had become.

Sometimes the stranger doesn't look so different. Sometimes she looks like your kid sister. Laura came to help with environmental education early on and stayed about three months. Within days of her arrival it became clear that Laura was wrestling with her own demons. In a word, she was needy and desperate for a listening ear. She latched onto me as her listening ear of choice. She found a rocker in our living room and when she wasn't outside helping with school programs or working in the garden, she was inside rocking in our rocking chair—waiting for me. Her neediness and its implications for me were complicated by the fact that I already had two very needy girls in my life—my own. Bryn was still quite young and therefore mostly oblivious, but Maya was preschool aged and wary enough to know that she had competition for my attention. Laura and Maya developed a sparring sibling rivalry that included, at one point, growling and temper tantrums on Maya's part.

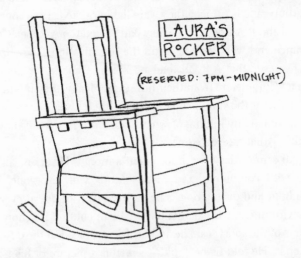

LAURA'S ROCKER

(RESERVED: 7PM – MIDNIGHT)

Under the strain I wanted to send Laura home. But she'd come from afar and her plane ticket had been booked, and though I found her taxing, I couldn't imagine rejecting her, thereby increasing her future neediness. And so I prayed. I prayed to have the courage to welcome this stranger. I also put up some modest boundaries—during daylit hours Maya got my attention first, but in the evenings when Maya had gone to bed and Markku was happily reading the news, I gave my attention to Laura.

I remember the first night of this new routine. I asked Laura if I could pray for her. It took everything in me to ask this simple question, as if the request were a physical lump in my throat. I didn't want to pray for her. I wanted to go to bed and curl up with a good book and leave her sitting on the rocking chair by herself. Mercifully I didn't, and, of course, she said yes. I can't recall what I prayed, but I remember the change it birthed. Not in her, but in me. I suddenly felt something akin to sympathy. My dislike softened into curiosity. Over the next couple of months we talked often. She cried, I listened or prayed, and affection grew. As I reached out I was changed. And bit by bit Laura changed too. Don't get me wrong, she didn't leave singing show tunes, but she did return home a bit more hopeful and a bit more *well* for having been listened to and accepted.

BOUNDARIES

Given the "successes" of Ali and Laura, it would be easy at this point to cast a rosy glow over the whole community living/welcoming the stranger enterprise, but it did come at a price. Sometimes that price got paid back in my own personal growth, as was the case with Laura, but sometimes that price was simply paid out in sleep deprivation, with no return benefit. Because we lived in an old farmhouse with creaky wood floors and because interns often kept different hours from our own, we were often awakened in the night to the sounds of interns coming to and fro. I remember one particular intern who set the record for night-time volume as she plodded up and down the hall at one in the morning—on what seemed like elephant feet—loudly banging the bathroom door open and shut a total of six times.

And sometimes the cost came in personal sanity, like the time I returned from cleaning the community kitchen at the "Main

House" and walked into my own kitchen only to find it overrun with interns baking cookies in a sea of flour, sugar, and dirty mixing bowls, all the while rocking out to seriously loud heavy-metalish music. (I tend toward muted folk in my musical taste and tidy kitchens in my aesthetic taste.)

After about two years of such occurrences I began to pay attention to the feeling of dread that seized me as soon as I got word that a short-term guest was arriving and would be occupying the bedroom opposite ours. The dread came not only from the anticipated lack of sleep, but also from the need for private space where we could "hole up" as a family and tend to the emotional needs of our growing girls. The solution came when we enlisted Markku's father—and A Rocha's volunteer builder extraordinaire—who in the span of two months threw up a wall and created a private space for our family. It was small, but very sweet and put me in mind of sailing on the Good Ship Ikea—everything neat and tidy and self-contained. It was perfect.

So for the next four years we still remained very much part of the A Rocha community, but with the bonus of one significant boundary in the form of a door behind which we could retreat when the need arose.

LETTING OUR LITTLE LIGHTS SHINE

Eugene Peterson tells the story of having a crush on a nun. The nun in question was his spiritual director, and he didn't really have a crush on *her*, but on her way of life. One day while meeting with her he was waxing eloquent about how wonderful it'd be to live such a life—in true community and simplicity—when the nun stopped him in his tracks.

She asked if he found being married easy.

He replied, that, well, no, it was the hardest thing he'd ever attempted—the hardest, he said, but the best. He explained that marriage was a continual process of learning to love and forgive, and that's always a hard process.

"Ah," said the nun. "Imagine, then, being married to thirty-two other people."

Anyone who has been married any length of time will tell you that the most challenging aspect of marriage is not coming to terms with one's spouse, but with *oneself.* It's the dross in one's own life that bubbles to the surface in the crucible of such intimacy that is so unattractive and must be dealt with if the marriage is to be healthy. In this way, marriage acts as a mirror, reflecting the imperfections we can hide from the rest of the world, but not from our partner and thus from ourselves. And if marriage is a mirror, then intentional community living is a house of mirrors. The trick to doing it semi-well is to keep loving and forgiving—especially oneself—in the midst of the grind of everyday life. But in order to love and forgive, one must be authentic.

CASTING OFF VEILS

One of the most poignant biblical passages concerning authenticity is Paul's discourse on the covenants of Grace and Law in 2 Corinthians 3:7–11. In this passage Paul encourages the Corinthians not to be like Moses who put on a veil when talking with the Israelites. It's a fascinating passage because Paul seems to fill in what the Old Testament leaves out. The event in question was the time just after Moses' second trip up Mount Sinai, where he encountered God and came down with the Ten Commandments (Exod 34:33–35).

Now, I had always thought Moses put the veil on when he talked to Israelites because they couldn't handle the glow, which they found too holy and overwhelming. But Paul contends that Moses put the veil on because he lacked boldness. Evidently, according to Paul, Moses didn't want the Israelites to think the glory was fading. The veil, in essence, was a mask, deceiving the Israelites into thinking something was true, when it really wasn't. Was Moses's bit of deception motivated by some sort of strategic leadership plan? Was it due to pride or insecurity? We don't know, but the point of the passage is that followers of Christ are under a new covenant of grace and in grace, there is no place for a veil. In fact, there is freedom—freedom to be unmasked.

Once we are unmasked, we are free to give God the glory, because only then do we reflect Christ's glory. Paul says just this as he extends the theme in verse 4:7: "But we have this treasure in earthen jars to show that this all-surpassing power is from God and not from us." The earthen jars he was referring to were common oil lamps found in the Corinthian market. With a small hole for a lighted wick that drew up the oil from within the clay, these lamps were fragile and broke easily, often containing cracks and blemishes. In contrast to more expensive lamps made of gold or bronze, the source of light was plainly obvious in these earthen pots. One might get confused or distracted by the glitter of gold, as the shining surface of the metal reflected the light, but surely there's no mistaking the flicker of a flame in a simple clay jar.

Of course our interns don't come to be unmasked. They come to study frogs or to plant ferns. The fact that they get to live and work alongside other frog and fern lovers is a bonus. What they don't realize, perhaps, is that inclusion is the beginning of transformation. Merely by setting foot into the A Rocha community they have been included in a family of sorts—a family full of cracked pots who are willing to let the light of God's love shine: a family who, on our best days, strives toward authenticity.

Robin came from England to study salamanders. She'd had an exceptionally hard early life and had been adopted out of a traumatic scenario at age twelve by a vicar and his wife. Though her adopted parents were caring and devout, she found church stodgy and irrelevant. She came to A Rocha with a chip on her shoulder where faith was concerned and worried that she wouldn't fit in. But to her own surprise, she found herself in a group of fun, interesting people who cared about the things she cared about—salamanders, frogs, and dragonflies most of all. Most importantly, she told me later, people at A Rocha were "real." The fact that most of those in the community professed a Christian faith she found both puzzling and intriguing.

The turning point in her opinions of what Christian faith could mean came one fall afternoon, while she was happily chopping vegetables with another intern, a committed and thoughtful Christian with a winsome personality. Suddenly, the latter dropped a butcher knife he'd been using to chop carrots. It glanced off his foot, and as it did, he let loose with a bugling, "F***!"

Robin was thrilled. And so encouraged. After witnessing this marvelous scene, she actually thought she might be open to exploring Christian faith for herself.

But there was a foil character to the Cheery Curser—a know-it-all fellow whose convictions were stunningly black and white. He could argue anyone into the ground on any point. He was a walking and talking encyclopedia. And he was always right. About everything. It didn't matter what the topic, whether it was the mating habits of the rough-skinned newt or the theology of predestination, he had the definitive say. The more gracious in our community made polite small talk *with* him, the rest of us made very wide circles *around* him.

The contrast between the swearing, authentic Christian and the iron-clad argumentative Christian was stark. The latter drove Robin absolutely batty. The former emboldened her to embrace her humanity—not as something she had to do away with in order to gain God's favor, but as something integral to who she was and even lovable to God.

CATCHING THOSE WHO COME

"Community is a net" was one of the favorite expressions of Jessica Nye Brouwer, A Rocha's accountant who joined us in our second year on site. Some are better at catching those who fall off the high wire act of life, and Jessica was one of those. Every time someone walked through the door into the Center's community space, she'd call out his or her name with an enthusiasm usually reserved for a long-lost relative. "Leah!!" she'd trumpet as if she hadn't seen me in weeks and my walking through the door was the greatest gift she could imagine. It was like a boisterous verbal embrace, and it was deeply encouraging. The rather humorous ballast to her clarion welcomes was the fact that in regular conversation she was a mumbler. We leaned in close when she spoke, not primarily because we were so enthralled by what she was saying—though most often what she said was quite enthralling—but because we couldn't for the life of us *hear* what she was saying. But, no matter, everyone put up with her mumbling because she shined acceptance and delight in people.

Others adept at "holding the net" were the Faws, followed by the Ewings, collectively known as the Center moles, not because they had bad eyesight, but because they lived (one family followed by the other) in a basement suite under the "Main House's" community space. A born dialoguer, Rick Faw is remembered by interns for late-night discussions. While his wife and children slept, he'd sneak back upstairs and stay up half the night exploring issues of faith, the environment, and sports with eager interns.

Jay and Milissa Ewing were with us for two years and served as Center Directors, relieving much of the burden of Center management from our shoulders (though Rick had already shouldered a good deal of it as well). I think most people's first impression of Jay was his hair. He had black Shirley Temple hair that bobbed in short ringlets on his head and was coveted by every woman who passed through A Rocha's doors. The second impression of Jay was his genuine friendliness, leading many to conclude that he might just be the friendliest person on earth. His personality was a great antidote to the typical scientist's, whose personality, in our experience, leans more toward the subdued. I recall many a meal when Jay was not present and the rest of us ate in ponderous silence.

Jay's wife was quieter, but equally kind. Coming from First Nations descent, she looked like a wholesome version of Cher. We were unduly proud of her ethnic profile and, truth be told, were often tempted to parade her out to newly arrived guests and say meaningfully, "Did we mention she's *Native?*"

Probably the one most consistent at holding the edges of the community net was Brian Marek, our Center cook and artist in residence. He was not systematic in his "catching" or mentoring of interns, he was simply present. He was primarily present in the kitchen, where he coached a steady stream of interns and volunteers in the fine art of local and gourmet cooking. While whipping up a mean crème brûlée, he could joke or wax philosophical depending on the need of his pupil. It was not surprising, therefore, that when interns left they were often most grateful for living in community and learning to cook—both Brian's domains.

Some are caught not so much by the people, but the place. It's healing just to be at an A Rocha Center, even if it's just for a few hours. And so we welcome the stranger even if he or she comes just a few hours per week. Some of those we welcome are part of the Early Psychosis Intervention (EPI) program. EPI is a service offered by the Fraser Health Authority through which young adults aged thirteen to thirty-five receive help in regaining their mental and emotional footing after their first psychotic episode. One way of creating normalcy is through volunteering in the community. EPI volunteers come each week to work in our garden alongside A Rocha staff and volunteers. For many participants—some of whom are still hospitalized and just out on "day passes"—their time at A Rocha is a first step toward mental and emotional wholeness. Of course, when offering hospitality to folks who've been through traumatic episodes, one doesn't want to overwhelm them with sappy enthusiasm or too much conversation, so generally we give them their space and allow Paul, our farmer, to work his relational magic with them. The rest of us try to give lots of long crinkly-eye smiles when they glance our way. But it's the place that works the

real magic. The chance to dig, pull, haul—to use their muscles under a clear or cloudy sky with a rooster crowing nearby—centers
these fragile folk in the tangible reality of creation.

THE CHALLENGES

One of the toughest parts of community life at an A Rocha Center, for the staff at least, is the turnover. Just when someone has
worked hard at dropping their mask they leave. We lived on-site
at the A Rocha Center for six years. In that time about one hundred interns and volunteers came to stay. When it was time for
someone to depart, Bryn and Maya developed the tradition of
racing down the driveway in pursuit of his or her exiting car, all
the while shouting and waving frantically. Usually our girls weren't
overly heartbroken by visitors' departures, but on one occasion, a
five-year-old Maya streaked down the driveway after a receding
blue minivan, wailing in despair, "Joyti!" Joyti was the ten-year-old
daughter of a couple who had volunteered for a few weeks, and she
had proven to be a considerate playmate—pushing Maya on the
swings, participating in tea parties, and playing endless hours of
tag on the lawn.

Fortunately for Maya, Joyti's family got a block down the
road and then suffered a flat tire. Her father, Simon, came stump-
ing back up the driveway a few minutes after their exit looking
like, well, looking like he'd just spent the morning packing up for a
cross-country trip only to get a flat tire a block out of the driveway.
Maya was thrilled and glowed in Joyti's briefly extended presence.

I generally enjoy being in the eye of the community living
storm, but I also appreciate the calm seas of familiar faces. I remember the heartbreak that lasted for weeks after our dear colleagues Melissa Ong and Daniel Tay returned to Singapore after
a two-year stint working as A Rocha filmmakers based out of our
Center. I could hardly walk by their room without getting teared
up. For interns and volunteers, living at A Rocha is often a summer
camp experience in its intensity and transformational impact, but
for the staff who need to send their kids to school, relate to their

families, pay bills, and achieve some semblance of an outside so-cial life, the emotional toll of welcoming and bidding farewell to a revolving door of people can be exhausting, especially when some of them take part of your heart with them when they go.

Sometimes it's not even the saying of goodbyes that becomes wearying. It's simply having the same conversation over and over. You'd be surprised, for example, how many times the what-does-an-animal-say-in-other-languages conversation makes the circuit at an environmental center. True, it is interesting to know that in Dutch a pig says "knor, knor"; in Finnish, "groin, groin"; and—how charming—in Japanese, "boo, boo"; but with each lap around the dinnertime conversation track, even these tasty morsels of information lose a bit of their zest.

ALL IN THE FAMILY

I've always been fascinated by rites of passage. Some aboriginal cultures practice a vision quest. Some Amish practice *rumspringa*, setting their sixteen-year-olds free to experiment in the "real" world. The Jewish tradition has its bar mitzvah. But one of my favorites involves a sort of family swap. Evidently, in some Native American cultures, when a child turns thirteen, he is sent to live with an aunt or other close relative for a spell. Though this tradition might seem like a way of preserving parental sanity in the face of teenage rebellion, the practice has a much more positive, child-empowering aspect. The practice is based on the assumption that as a young person transitions from childhood to adulthood, he needs a new context and new responsibilities. He is still part of the family, but is given the freedom to live into his changing skin without the strictures of his childhood identity.

The A Rocha community is a bit like this. In essence, our environmental center has been a place where interns can grow up. Of course our center is more than this, since thousands come and just dip their toe in the A Rocha waters for an afternoon or day. But for those who come for extended periods of time, the benefit derived from adult responsibilities, as well as the freedom to explore ideas and convictions, can be transformational, especially since the context for these new responsibilities and freedoms occurs within the embrace of the A Rocha family. The key to growth for everyone who comes is the atmosphere of safety that is intentionally fostered. There's been transformation because we try to make the A Rocha Center a safe place where you can take off your mask and be real—where you can even sing an aria if you are so inclined.

And some do.

Cathy was a stereotypical science nerd, with big round glasses and a surprising soprano voice. Her voice was surprising not because it was so good (though it was), but because Cathy would employ it when you least expected it. The girl loved arias. Her favorite was that sequence in *Little Mermaid* when Ariel surges from the water and sings mounting crescendos of "Ahhhhhh, ahhhhhh's." Cathy loved that bit. And she was shameless in her choice of venue and audience. You'd be standing in the kitchen chopping vegetables, minding your own business, when all of a sudden a clarion voice would burst forth from behind you, nearly causing you to slice off your finger. "Ahhh-hhhahhhh!" she'd sing as you gripped the counter and panted from the shock of it all. My personal strategy for handling these startling concerts was to meekly go on with my chopping with the faux air of a Zen master. The problem came when she finished—I never knew whether to clap or look at my toes.

But that's community for you—learning to love and stay hospitable, even when someone sneaks into your cozy personal space with the freedom to sing an aria.

5

Naming, but Not Claiming

The last word in ignorance is the man who says of an animal or plant, "What good is it?" If the land mechanism as a whole is good, then every part is good, whether we understand it or not. If the biota, in the course of eons, has built something we like but do not understand, then who but a fool would discard seemingly useless parts? To keep every cog and wheel is the first precaution of intelligent tinkering.

ALDO LEOPOLD

FUNNY THING ABOUT BIODIVERSITY—IT'S great in principle, but when things start to get too, well, *diverse*, one's feelings on the matter get a bit muddled. Allow me to explain. Back in 2005, A Rocha's Environmental Center had the usual diversity of biological life: chickens, cows, and a myriad of plants and veggies on the farmy bit; frogs, salamanders, newts, shrews, and at least forty species of birds in the wetland/forest bit; and homo sapiens in the shape of staff, volunteers, interns, and school children throughout. We celebrate this kind of biodiversity. That year, however, things got too diverse—too diverse by two species. The first, *Canis latrans*, was spotted the previous spring, drawn by our chickens, who being free range apparently seemed a free smorgasbord for our canine nemesis. The coyotes (for that's what they were) picked off two of our lovely heritage breed chickens, most notably Miss Mullet, a Black Polish cross with a crazy hairdo for whom we all mourned. So the rest of the chickens went back into the coop. But the farm was so much farmier with the "girls" scratching about, and so we let them out again. In short—and in short order—the coyote took three more chickens. Now the four that remained were only let out under the strictest supervision. But since the allure of chicken-sitting wears off after about fifteen minutes, they spent most of their time behind bars. Alas, what can you do when you live in a zoo?

The second species to appear uninvited that year was *Rattus rattus* (that's really its Latin name). They took up residence in our basement that fall when the weather turned chilly. After chewing up numerous plastic buckets and figuring out quickly what the rat traps were all about, they took advantage of renovations on the main floor to sneak up into *our* living space. By the evidence they left, they boldly scurried up the stairs, visited every room in the house, and even started building a nest in our green corduroy couch. This last atrocity occurred while we were away for a week, and, needless to say, shot us into serious rat-eradication frenzy, which we eventually won.

To our shame, I must admit that we used the appearance of these two species to our unfair parental advantage. When Maya (aged four at the time) showed signs of dashing without permission from our house to visit the interesting interns at the "Main House," we casually would chirp, "Watch out for coyotes," which, of course, sent her scampering back to our sides. And when Bryn (then two) sauntered into the living room with a crumbly piece of toast in hand, we'd lightly draw for her the connection between crumbs and the onslaught of hungry rats. And so in their impressionable minds, coyotes were beasts to be feared above all others, and rats were so resourceful that at the mere scent of something delicious they flew from the basement to snatch the crumbs falling from one's mouth. Law and order in the here and now versus a battery of counseling sessions for our girls years in the future—it was a tough call.

SAVING SALMON

Of course, in reality, we are all for biodiversity. A Rocha is a conservation organization, after all, and the attempt to record and preserve the variety of the earth's biological life is at the core of all conservation work everywhere. To help assess the situation the International Union for Conservation Nature (IUCN) has developed the IUCN Red List of Threatened Species (www.iucnredlist.org), compiling studies and statistics from over eleven thousand experts in various fields of biology. Their findings point to species extinction rates that are between one thousand to ten thousand times above the natural background rates. According to their research, we are currently facing the possible extinction of 13 percent of birds, 25 percent of mammals, and 41 percent of amphibians worldwide.

So we work in conservation, and because A Rocha Canada was born on the Pacific coast, our conservation efforts began with that iconic Pacific creature—the salmon. Few animals on Canada's West Coast symbolize the link between forest and ocean ecosystems better than Pacific salmon. It's the old hip-bone-is-connected-to-the-thigh-bone song and dance, but with an ecological twist, all done against the backdrop of one of creation's greatest migration cycles.

Beginning their lives in freshwater lakes, rivers and streams, the juvenile salmon spend a few months to a few years (depending on the species) in fresh water before they head out to sea, where they will grow up to twenty-three kilograms (fifty pounds). The fare that enables them to pack on 98 percent of their adult weight includes plankton, shrimp, anchovies, and herring, to name a few. At some point in each salmon's life, an instinctual bell goes off, telling it to return home. For some species this is relatively simple, since they have not ventured farther than 240 kilometers (150 miles) from their home stream, but for others, like the Chinook, who often travel as far as 4,000 kilometers (2,500 miles) out to sea, it is an astounding feat. Not only do the vast majority of salmon migrate back to the very stream in which they were spawned, most make it within a few hundred meters of their hatching place. Scientists are unclear how salmon navigate home, but evidently they use their sense of smell since a fish with a plugged nose can't find its way back.

Once again in fresh water, the drama heightens. Females' bodies bulge with eggs. Males are often battered, with humped backs and torn fins, as they make the strenuous race against time to the spawning beds. The last leg of a salmon's life might seem macabre to those wanting to anthropomorphize their homecoming, but the spawning and subsequent death of salmon is one of the great connecting agents between the ecology of the ocean and that of the coastal forest of western Canada. Some twenty-two species of mammals and birds feed directly on living or dead salmon, from grizzlies to bald eagles to stoneflies. According to the Pacific Salmon Foundation, a total of 190 different species depend on salmon for survival. And so the cycle goes, as nutrients from a saltwater shrimp are transferred to a migrating Chinook, who loses the spawning race to a hungry grizzly, who leaves his droppings at the base of a Douglas-fir seedling, which grows to a towering height, thanks to the annual influx of fertilizer that coincides with the salmon run. Everyone scratches his or her head and wonders how that tree got so darn big, never dreaming it had anything to do with a measly shrimp!

But hazards abound for the Pacific salmon. Foremost among them are urbanization and resource extraction, which both lead to the loss of habitat. A Rocha has worked to protect and restore salmon habitat to ensure that this amazing creature continues to thrive. In our early days in North Vancouver, our church basement office looked out on Coleman Creek, which supports a variety of wildlife, including Coho salmon. It was natural, therefore, to begin a monitoring program through spawner and fry surveys.

And then we moved to the Little Campbell River watershed. The Little Campbell is an urban and rural jewel and has been named by the Outdoor Recreation Council one of B.C.'s top twelve endangered rivers. It's relatively small, stretching a mere thirty kilometers in length, but it spans two biogeoclimatic zones—Coastal Western Hemlock and Coastal Douglas-fir, and, most importantly, its estuary opens out into Canada's most significant Important Bird Area: Boundary Bay. The variety of human activity along its course means the Little Campbell is subject to stresses such as deforestation and silting, pollution from agricultural and industrial products, waste from animal husbandry, habitat loss from channeled tributaries and water withdrawal, and uncontrolled flashes from surface run-off. Phew! It's no wonder the river is threatened.

"But for all this," to quote Gerard Manley Hopkins, "nature is never spent." Despite habitat degradation, the Little Campbell River and its watershed continues to host hundreds of species, some of which are recognized as critically threatened, like the Red-legged Frog (*Rana aurora*) and Oregon Forestsnail (*Allogona townsendiana*). The river is also home to Coho, Chinook, and Chum salmon, as well as Steelhead and Cutthroat trout, each of which species is in various stages of stress. Being a small river, the numbers of fish are not huge, but combined with the thousands of streams that reach the ocean along B.C.'s coasts, it helps provide habitat for a considerable proportion of the salmon biomass in British Columbia and, according to a 2005 report by the Raincoast Conservation Foundation, likely a far greater proportion of salmon genetic diversity.

We've taken a two-pronged approach to the care for the river and the greater watershed. The first is habitat enhancement and restoration. The second is conservation science research. Habitat enhancement and restoration is basically a fancy way of saying pulling weeds and planting plants. Those who've studied ecology understand that "weed" in this case is code for "invasive species," an issue high on their environmental radars, but we artsy types have been slow in coming up to speed on this threat to biodiversity. If you fall in this latter camp here's the skinny on the issue. Because they come from afar, some introduced species have no natural predators or competitors in their new ecosystems and thus reproduce without check, leaving a "desert" for indigenous species whose prey, soil, or forage has been consumed by these newcomers.

The plague of Scotch Broom on Vancouver Island is a good case study for the potentially dire consequences of introducing non-native species. Back in 1850 Captain Walter Grant, yearning for the sights and smells of his native Edinburgh, planted a handful of Scotch Broom seeds on his property north of Victoria. Three seeds germinated. One hundred years later Scotch Broom had become a scourge—filling gullies, covering hillsides, blanketing fields, and choking out native species like Douglas-fir and Garry Oak. Each plant can produce up to thirty-five hundred seed pods which, when dry, explode, shooting up to forty thousand seeds per plant up to five meters in every direction. This is one noxious weed!

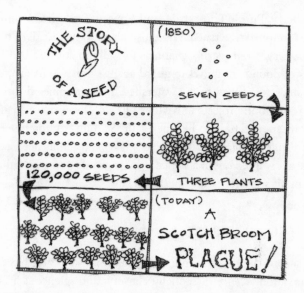

Now, of course, not every introduced species finds itself on the most (un)wanted list—apple trees, for example, generally stay put—but a quick glance at the "baddies" in one's own ecosystem can offer surprises. Here are a few of the worst in the Vancouver area:

Animals	Plants
American Bullfrog	English Ivy
Domestic Cat	False Lamium
European Rabbit	Giant Hogweed
Goldfish	Himalayan Blackberry
Grey Squirrel	Police Helmet
Norway Rat	Purple Loosestrife
Red-eared Sliders (a.k.a. turtles)	Scotch Broom

Funny how many of these fall in the pet or potted-plant category. Now, we haven't gone on any bunny hunts, but thanks to an endless army of volunteers working under the oversight of our former and intrepid Science Director, Glen Carlson, and our new Environmental Stewardship Officer, Christy Juteau, we have pulled, cut, and removed literally tons of English Ivy, Himalayan

Blackberry, Purple Loosestrife, and Canary Reed Grass from the Little Campbell watershed. We've also planted truckloads of native plants, carved out rearing channels for salmon fry, and laid hundreds of pounds of gravel to guard against erosion. In fact, each year since we moved to the watershed, we've completed three or four restoration projects in partnership with local municipalities, landowners, and funders like the Pacific Salmon Foundation. Each plant planted and each truckload of gravel spread has been a missional act worked out in a stance of hope as we've cooperated with God in his work to "makes all things new."

NAMING THE BEAST

Our second approach to our watershed's preservation has been conservation science. Essentially conservation science is a fancy way of saying learning names and making lists, the idea being that you can't protect a thing if you don't know it's out there—or if you don't know its population is in decline. So we learn names and make lists. It's biblical, actually. Doesn't the creation narrative say that this was one of Adam's first jobs—naming the animals? And didn't Jesus tell his followers to "consider the birds of the air"? Learning a creature's name can be quite exciting, even for those who've been in the name game for a long time. I remember hosting Dave Bookless, founder of A Rocha UK and an amateur ornithologist with a very long "life list" of bird species. At one point he was desperate to call home; I learned why when I later heard him exclaim to his wife, "I just saw a robin!"

At the risk of wandering too far down this rabbit trail, I would like to suggest that naming is not only valuable for the nuts and bolts of conservation science databases, but is valuable in a fundamentally aesthetic and even moral way. Learning a name gives worth to the thing named. Think how "unknown" and undervalued you feel when someone can't remember your name. In theological terms naming is the first step in moving from an "I-It" relationship with something or someone to an "I-Thou" relationship, a relationship where a person or creature or even an object becomes known not just for its usefulness, but for its innate worth. It's the first step in the kind of understanding that leads to caring.

Moving from philosophy to trivia, I offer the following names which represent category groupings that fall in the literary rather than scientific nomenclature camp. You've heard of a gaggle of geese, but how about:

A siege of herons
A charm of goldfinches
A mess of iguanas
A muster of peafowl
A murmuration of starlings
A herd of swans
A venue of vultures
A murder of crows
And a whoop of gorillas

But I digress.

In our effort to protect and preserve the biodiversity of the Little Campbell watershed, our staff and interns carry out a wide variety of monitoring projects. A great boon to this aspect of our work has been Environment Canada's Science Horizons Youth Internship program, which has allowed us to hire a number of young scientists fresh out of university for nine-month internships. Our first Science Horizons intern, Rachel Krause, undertook two major monitoring projects on the river and subsequently submitted two hefty reports to the B.C. Ministry of Environment and Environment Canada respectively. Her first project, a benthic invertebrate survey, aimed to gain a holistic picture of stream health by recording the diversity and abundance of benthic invertebrates—that's "bottom-dwelling bugs" to the uninitiated—in the Little Campbell. Her studies set the groundwork for subsequent invertebrate studies carried out by A Rocha's conservation interns over the past five years. And they have been cursing her name ever since! After all, an afternoon staring through a microscope in an attempt to identify a never ending parade of annelid worms can drive even the most hard-core biologist around the bend. But then nobody said scientific research was going to be glamorous.

Rachel's second project certainly wasn't since it involved, well, poo. Okay, fecal coliforms, if we're being technical. Rachel's study was part of a larger water quality monitoring project commissioned by Environment Canada and the Shared Waters Alliance in response to a rising concern regarding fecal contamination of Boundary Bay. Her report, coupled with her work on invertebrates, went a long way in helping the Little Campbell get that "Most Endangered River" status.

TAMING THE SHREW

For the record, we don't limit all our conservation interns and volunteers to the study of bugs and poo. We are an Environmental Center, after all, and have encouraged environmental studies of a wide variety. Over the years, A Rocha folk have carried out monitoring surveys on hummingbirds, herons, raptors, amphibians, dragonflies, fresh water mussels, and small mammals, to name a few. The latter was the brainchild of Martin Lings, a loveable English intern who holds the record for having slept in the most buildings at A Rocha's first center: main house, farmhouse, tree house, log cabin, and quonset hut, for those counting. His decision to study small mammals was spurred by the dream of discovering, or rather rediscovering, the elusive Pacific Water Shrew (*Sorex bendirii*), a provincially red-listed (i.e., endangered) species of shrew that hasn't been spotted in the Little Campbell watershed since the mid-1980s.

Pacific Water Shrew

Once he'd done a bit of research on live-trapping methodology and had procured the necessary permits—yes, you need a permit to trap a field mouse if it's for scientific purposes—he set up five traps in strategic locations around the Center property. These traps were hardly high tech. Actually, they looked more like trash than the stuff of scientific research. Comprised essentially of little cardboard fences draped in clear plastic with a sunken bucket at one end, the idea was that in the course of scurrying along the forest floor, a small mammal would run into one of these aforementioned fences, travel along the length of it and then fall into the bucket. The point wasn't to kill the creatures, but to record numbers, species, measurements, and genders and then let them go. To ensure the survival of these little rodents, Martin set his alarm for every hour on the hour through the night—small mammals being nocturnal—during his forty-eight-hour survey.

I, of course, slept through the whole thing, but I did spot Martin late one evening, field guide and notebook in hand, headlamp blazing on his forehead, and, I must admit, he did strike quite the *National Geographic* pose. Unfortunately, scientific glory eluded him, for not a single Pacific Water Shrew found its way into his traps. Perhaps, sadly, this species has indeed vanished from our watershed. Or perhaps, the very last one of its kind took a right at that old stump in the A Rocha forest instead of a left, and thereby missed out on the excitement of landing in Martin's bucket. Whatever the case, Martin did find quite a few other shrews and voles, making the study a real success. My personal favorites were the Vagrant Shrew and the Creeping Vole. (Who names these things, little old ladies!?) But Martin was most impressed with the forty-three Trowbridge Shrews he caught.

He was not, however, impressed by the one that died. Finding its lifeless body in his bucket and not wanting its death to have been in vain, he decided that, for the sake of science, he would preserve its skeleton. So he tucked it into a little Ziploc bag, put in the freezer (where it joined a number of other Ziplocked creatures, including two hummingbirds and a Barred Owl—all tossed in amongst bags of peas and corn and chopped spinach) and contemplated the fine art of taxidermy. He decided the best way to get at those bones was to boil the whole shrew down. He therefore retrieved it from the freezer, threw it in a pot of water, and set it on the stove to boil. And then promptly forgot all about it. Three hours later the wife of our Capital Campaign Chairman dropped in to say hello. When no one answered her knock she let herself in and was met by the most noxious smell ever to have filled her nostrils. The alarm was raised and Tiina, our office manager, came running in a mad rush to discover the source of this incredibly potent odor. Martin, by the way, was nowhere to be found. Tiina followed her nose to the stove, eyed the offending pot, and, with a high degree of trepidation, lifted lid. There, etched in a charcoal grizzle, was the blackened snout and the burnt outline of what had once been a Trowbridge Shrew—a crime scene in rodent minia- ture. So much for posterity.

THE UGLY BUG BALL

Despite this one spectacular failure, it is our conservation work that undergirds everything else we do at A Rocha. While we be- lieve in the importance of advocacy and activism, what makes A Rocha unique among faith-based conservation groups is our dedication to on-the-ground conservation and research. Yes, we train, educate, inspire, and encourage, but we also pull, plant, study, and restore. This kind of work isn't flashy, as the bug-study- ing interns will tell you, but it also isn't a flash-in-the-pan since we are committed to specific places over the long term. This kind of commitment requires getting to know our neighbors, both human and non-human, and persistently working for the health of all.

If it is our commitment to hands-on conservation that makes us unique in the faith-based environmental world, then it is do- ing it well that gives us credibility in the secular conservation world. In this regard I'm reminded of the Ugly Bug Ball, which we've hosted every second year for the past six years. The Ball isn't really a ball (though there is a dance in the evening where every- one comes dressed as their favorite invertebrate), but a full day of encouragement, knowledge sharing, and appreciation put on by the Department of Fisheries and Oceans Canada (DFO) and the Pacific Streamkeepers Federation. The party is a way of thanking volunteers from all over the Greater Vancouver Area for their efforts in stewarding their local salmon-bearing streams. Basically, DFO throws the party and A Rocha provides the setting. This might seem like an odd partnership—a government entity and a faith-based organization—and, truth be told, I think the DFO officers initially thought so as well.

The scouting delegation they sent to see if our property would make a good site certainly emerged from their big blue diesel trucks looking circumspect. Markku met them in the driveway and grasped the nettle straight away, asking what they thought about us being a Christian group. A couple of them admitted that it made them a little nervous. Markku assured them he wasn't going to whack them on the side of their heads with a Bible. A Rocha's conservation work wasn't a front for proselytizing, he said. They began to breathe a bit easier. He went on to explain how doing good conservation work was an outworking of our Christian calling to steward creation. They got that. Then Markku rattled off some of our projects, things like our participation in the B.C. Coastal Shorebirds survey and, of course, our work on the Little Campbell River. By the end of their visit a date was set for the first Ugly Bug Ball and everyone was smiling and slapping backs.

The feelings of good will and admiration are mutual and have grown over the six years of partnering. We enjoy the music, games, and presentations when all those ugly bugs descend on the Center and our guests enjoy the property as they tool down the forest path and meander around the garden. Some even take an interest in who we are and what we're doing. They even weigh in with advice and helpful suggestions. My favorite came from a white-bearded, Hawaiian shirt-clad guy, who suggested—in all seriousness—that we could get a lot more volunteers out to work in our garden if we offered "Gardening in the Nude" volunteer days. Yes, well, it certainly could get exciting should the coyotes show up.

GOD'S SURPRISE

The most significant feather in our conservation cap has come more recently. I was strolling across the lawn when one of our summer interns came scurrying by carrying a bucket. When I asked what it held she showed me a grey, wide-lipped fish swimming in a few inches of water. Her voice betrayed her excitement as she related that she was off to the program office to identify it.

Turns out it was a Salish Sucker—an endangered species. Not seen in our watershed since the 1970s, this species had been considered "extirpated" in the Little Campbell River system. Needless to say, her find was a very big deal!

When I asked later about the experience of discovering an endangered species, she told me the story of the day. Obviously a girl who enjoyed an intimate relationship with God, she said that upon waking she had felt like God was saying to her, "I have a surprise for you today." She went about her day, doing interny things, wondering all the while when the "surprise" was going to show up. Near the end of the afternoon, she toured some visitors around the A Rocha property and down to the pond where she could check a fish trap which was being used as part of an invasive species monitoring project. In fact, this was to be her last "check" of the season. As she bent to pull the trap out of the water she felt God saying, "Here's your surprise."

Her eyes brightened as she told me how she lifted the wire cage and found, not a Pumpkinseed fish or one of the other invasive species she'd been catching all summer, but a strange fish that looked too big to even fit through the opening of the trap. She knew immediately that it was something special.

I grinned widely. "Wow! Amazing!" I said. "How fantastic!" And, in the inner sanctum of my mind, I thought, *What a whacko*!

I thought this even though I believe wholeheartedly in God's care for all of his creation.

In hindsight I think I viewed this fish-finding intern as a whacko for two reasons:

1. To "hear" God speaking so directly is weird. How presumptuous! But my own experiences in contemplative prayer had demonstrated that God is quite capable of interacting on a very personal level. (Funny how God's interactions seem so bizarre in other people's lives but not in one's own.)

2. To assume that God cares about a sucker fish is weird. Sure, I believe, as that old song goes, that "His eye is on the sparrow." And when it comes to endangered species I am easily convinced that his eye is on the Panda, and the Sumatran Tiger, and even the Vancouver Island Marmot. But on the Salish Sucker? A bottom-feeding, wide-mouthed fish with big lips? *God's* eye is on such an ignoble, unattractive creature? That's weird.

And so I'm left with the question, who's the whacko? Maybe God's the whacko—a God who risks his reputation to earnest interns and middle-aged contemplatives. A God who fixes his eye on the humble, the overlooked, the ugly. A God whose eye is on the Sucker.

Turns out God's attention on that Sucker has been very good news for A Rocha's conservation program. It has boosted our profile as a conservation organization (discovering an endangered species is evidently your ticket into the environmental stewardship big leagues) and brought higher profile to the Little Campbell watershed and the threats to its viability. All this comes none too soon as development continues in the area at a significant rate, often without thoughtful consideration of environmental impacts. The whole episode seems worthy of some sort of theme music ("Here I come to save the day!"), where God suddenly shows up on the scene and proves to be the *machina dei* in the drama of our story.

6

Windows into Wonder

We care for only what we love. We love only what we know.
We truly know only what we experience.

STEVEN BOUMA-PREDIGER

STEVEN BOUMA-PREDIGER'S PARADIGM OF experience translating into knowledge, knowledge into love and love into care—encapsulated in the quote above—is the foundation for A Rocha's education work. We didn't come up with this brilliant formula; educators everywhere are drawing the same pedagogical conclusions. After all, it doesn't take a rocket scientist to figure out that learning about the natural world happens best *in* the natural world. Kids especially "get" this. Ask any child about her favorite school activity and, odds are, you'll hear a lot about recess. Pressed for something a bit more educational, she might scrunch her brow into a tight little knot until finally it dawns on her: "Field trips, yep, field trips, like to the Aquarium or that Ecology Center." Surely it's not merely the absence of pens and papers, tests and florescent lights that makes these two activities so universally appealing. Could it simply be that both activities happen, for the most part, *outside*? That, when studying the forest ecosystems, the child was invited to touch a real live three-dimensional tree rather than just the commercial two-dimensional byproduct of a tree: a worksheet.

The trick, of course, is getting kids outside—into what writer and naturalist Bob Pyle calls "places of initiation"—where they can experience creation first hand, preferably with caring adults who can model and share their wonder at what they see and experience. Actually, the trick is *keeping* them outside. Somehow, through lack of access to outdoors or through being plugged in to too many gadgets for too many hours, a child's love for the natural world is dampened, goes dormant, and is even extinguished.

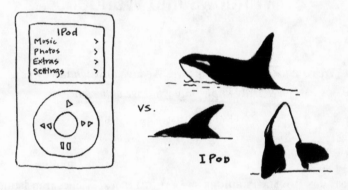

Richard Louv, author of *Last Child in the Woods*, picks up on this theme, suggesting that today's youth are in a sorry state—physically, mentally, and emotionally. The causes are many, but a leading culprit, he contends, is children's disconnect from the natural world. The malady even has a name: "nature deficit disorder." The numbers display this disconnect in all its starkness: only 6 percent of children aged nine to thirteen play outside on their own in a typical week. You don't have to be a granola-munching Luddite to realize that something is seriously amiss here! Besides the educational worth of getting out into the Great Outdoors—a 2005 study by the California

Department of Education showed that students in outdoor science programs scored 27 percent above their peers in traditional indoor programs—there is the long-term conservation benefit of a generation of kids who love creation and thus care for it.

LEARNING IN THE GREAT OUTDOORS

Therefore, A Rocha's education programs happen outside. They are light on dogma and rich in experience and build on children's innate love and fascination for creation. Ironically, our first foray into environmental education began in East Vancouver, in a neighborhood decidedly urban that boasts one of the lowest per capita incomes in all of Canada. For three years we ran *Explore Outdoors in the City*, a week-long summer day camp that reached out to "youth at risk" in this inner-city neighborhood. We chose this urban setting because, though Vancouver is well known for its spectacular scenery (every license plate on every car once declared "Beautiful British Columbia"), many people, especially the children of those living on the economic margins, cannot easily get into the countryside or wilderness. It also helped that the Chair of our board lived there with his wife, who was a pastor at Grandview Calvary Baptist, a church with a strong sense of social justice and a large activity room that they offered for day camp headquarters. The first year, Markku and our colleague, Patrick, ran the show, which meant they did everything from singing silly songs to leading daily excursions to Trout Lake Park a few blocks away. They even served as cooks for the hot dog lunches. (Why we served hot dogs is still a mystery!) Many of the kids were from foster families and obviously had lived tough lives. One particular boy spent much of the indoor time hunkered under a chair in a corner. If anyone approached to woo him out, he shouted expletives of the most vulgar kind. So Markku and Patrick let him be and invited him to participate as he felt able.

The remarkable thing was how this boy and his fellow day campers transformed when taken to the park. Granted, one is not likely to see elk or even a trout in Trout Lake Park, but the day campers did see lots of birds and bugs. There were bugs in the grass, bugs under the swing sets, bugs on the pathways. After a couple hours of acquiring new radars for these ubiquitous creatures, walking back to the church became a bug hunt. It was as if these kids had new eyes—ants were suddenly creatures to be shepherded, not crushed. Now, we A Rochaites aren't so concerned about protecting ants, per se, though we would certainly throw ourselves in the path of a wayward foot if the ant in question were the last of its species. The thing we are very concerned about is a child's attitude toward creation. If he wantonly crushes ants for the fun of it, odds are he won't be too concerned about the suffering and demise of larger species, including, studies have shown, his own.

With these inner-city day camps under our belts, we felt ready to expand our educational horizons. But Markku and Patrick were busy and after that first year, they were unable to run an environmental education program on top of administration, fundraising, and conservation work. We were tremendously blessed, therefore, when Heather Robinson and Ruth DesCotes joined our team. Both had a passion for environmental education and years of experience. They, along with volunteers and interns, took on the summer day camps and, once we moved to the Environmental Study Center, expanded A Rocha's educational repertoire to include school-sponsored field trips and special community outreach days.

Heather and Ruth—the "professionals"—confirmed what we had supposed instinctively: environmental education of lasting worth must be based on real encounters with creation which inspire and transform the participant. The environmental movement as a whole is coming to this realization as well, recognizing that the last thirty years of information dissemination—much of it in the form of dire statistics and doomsday forecasts—hasn't, for the most part, caused people to change the way they act. The fault lies not in the statistics, but in the fact that these statistics are just tiny sound bites in the cacophony of information that reach North American ears every day. As Neil Postman, the late and great sociologist, pointed out, North American media has turned information into entertainment, rendering it impotent when it comes to motivating change. We live in a deluge of information—awash in statistics that should have us running hell-bent through the streets to some constructive action. But we don't. It seems that fear tactics and empirical knowledge have a short shelf life when it comes to inspiring change. What lasts is wonder.

Wonder happens best in "wonderful" places, which is why it was such a boon to our education program to move to an Environmental Center. The ten acres of wetlands, forest, and fields allowed children to dip nets into ponds and pull out real, live tadpoles, dig fingers into freshly tilled dirt, and stand silently in a cedar grove to identify bird calls.

BEYOND THE ALLEGORICAL

Summer camps offer another venue for wonder. Early on in our history, A Rocha began partnerships with a variety of Christian camps in B.C., Alberta and Manitoba. Because of their location in often breathtaking surroundings, summer camps are a logical venue for A Rocha's work. Unfortunately, many camps have used creation as merely a beautiful backdrop for campfire sing-a-longs or a resource for water skiing or trail riding. Some camps go a bit further, using their stunning settings as spiritual capital, valuable in allegorically illustrating spiritual truths. That beautiful sunset, for example, represents God's delight; that storm cloud—his power; that trillium flower—his care and attention to the beauty of detail, and so on. Don't get me wrong, I think there is often merit in this sort of association game. Indeed, as the old hymn goes, "This is my Father's world, in the rustling grass I hear him pass, he speaks to me everywhere." Just recently Markku had an experience that seems straight from the hand of a God who delights in the allegorical.

To appreciate the significance of Markku's experience, you should know that we had just been talking about the Kingfisher, which in Celtic Christianity is associated with the Holy Spirit—evidently because they were constantly swooping out of nowhere, taking all those St. Aidans and St. Bridgettes by surprise. Oh, and because they hover over water. So, after our theological and historical musings, Markku trotted off to the beach for a walk. After about a half an hour he came to a large rock on which stood twelve Oystercatchers—those dramatic black shorebirds with shockingly red beaks and equally shocking red eyes and legs. They were all very busy pecking away at mussels and, as I mentioned, there were twelve. He watched for a moment and then realized that just to the right of the Oystercatchers were three Great Blue Herons doing what all herons everywhere seem to do—watching. By now Markku was drawing all sorts of allegorical connections. Here were the twelve disciples hard at work, oblivious to all else around them, even the Trinity that stood sentinel watching over them. Markku watched the Oysteratchers a few more seconds and then turned back to the herons to find a truncated Trinity—one of the herons had flown off without his notice. So he thought, "All I need now is a Kingfisher." And what do you think swooped in and hovered right overhead those busy Oystercatchers? A Kingfisher. No kidding.

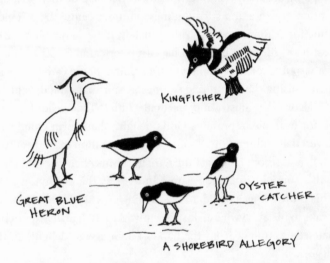

KINGFISHER

GREAT BLUE
HERON

OYSTER
CATCHER

A SHOREBIRD ALLEGORY

I need stories like this one, not only to bolster my faith in and understanding of God, but also because I'm a bit of a cynic at heart. I really do get the warm fuzzies from stories like Markku's, but I must admit I am also wary of them. I can't help wondering why the camp directors of the world leave out creation's darker side in their allegorical equations. Where are the rats, head lice, and tarantulas in all their musings? I suspect they are absent because God might not look so pretty from the vantage of creation's underbelly. To be equitable, a safer theological tack might let nature be nature rather than an illustration grab bag. Instead, one might "use" one's creation capital, whether it be a farm, beach, or wilderness trail, as a place for exploration and discovery—a place to really know—rather than just a backdrop for a more spiritual quest. We proposed just this to a number of Christian camps and all have been gamely enthusiastic.

Our pioneer camp in this partnership was, in fact, a Pioneer camp—Pioneer Pacific, an Intervarsity camp on Thetis Island. We employed two summer education interns, Alison Gratz and Christy Juteau, who quickly became known as "the A Rocha girls." They devised an *Explore Outdoors* program centered on experiencing the seashore, ponds, and woods of camp—essentially, glorified nature walks. Alison and Christy were initially a bit worried they might not have any takers since the choice *of* and involvement *in* activities at Pioneer Pacific is left entirely up to each individual camper. Nobody is required to do anything they deem boring or stupid or sissy. Now, you'd think a nature walk couldn't compete with sailing or water skiing or mountain biking, but by the end of the summer Alison and Christy's *Explore Outdoors* sessions were just as populated as these more adrenaline producing activities.

What made environmental education so enticing, you ask? They licked slugs. Why did they lick slugs, you ask? Because slug slime is an anesthetic: one lick and your tongue goes numb. Very cool. The slug licking was just one way campers got up close and personal with creation, and it reinforced the fact that one must employ one's senses and powers of observations to really get to know the natural world.

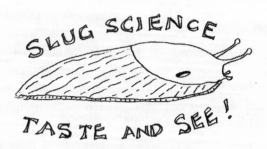

SLUG SCIENCE

TASTE AND SEE !

The other big hit was pond dipping which, as we've seen at our environmental center, can be a thrilling experience. To many, even a wild ride behind a speed boat can't compare with catching a salamander with your bare hands.

GETTING THE FACTS STRAIGHT

Experience of creation is made more powerful, more transformational, even more wonderful when substantiated with a few facts. I know, I said experience was *the* thing, but knowing what you're looking at certainly helps enrich that experience. Ironically, most environmental education curriculum in the classroom deals with ecosystems far removed from children's everyday lives. Kids in New Mexico learn about rain forests in Brazil, while students in Brazil learn about the tundra of the Arctic. Wouldn't it make sense to learn about the natural history and ecology of one's own place? Wouldn't it help me appreciate my own ecosystem if I knew the names of the birds singing in the trees outside my own front door? Loren Wilkinson, one of the grandfathers of the Christian environmental movement, has adapted a little quiz to help one get to know one's place.

Where on Earth are you?
(Fifteen questions about Your Place)

1. Trace the water you drink from precipitation to tap.

2. Describe the soil around your home.

3. Name five native edible plants in your area and their season(s) of availability.

4. From what direction do winter storms generally come in your region?

5. Where does your garbage go?

6. How long is the growing season where you live?

7. Name five trees in your area. Are any of them native?

8. Name five resident birds in your area.

9. What primary geological event or process influenced the land form where you live?

10. From where you are reading this, point north.

11. What spring wildflower is consistently among the first to bloom where you live?

12. What kinds of rocks and minerals are found in your area?

13. What were the primary subsistence techniques of the cultures(s) that lived in your area before you?

14. How many people live next door to you? What are their names?

15. What is the largest wild region in your area?

Of course, the best way to really ace this quiz is to visit the reservoir, dump, or farm for oneself. And so, we're back at experience. Again, we must get out of the classroom and away from the TV screen and venture outside. But most of us don't, even when it would be easy. I know from my own experience as a teacher that it's a lot simpler to keep students at their desks, scribbling down facts for the upcoming test, rather than turning them loose in the real world. It's easier, but not necessarily better.

LEARNING TO SEE

There was a wetland in the back of the school property where I taught, and to this wetland I led my ninth-grade English class one morning. The thick cover of cottonwoods and alders made the noise of traffic seem like the murmur of a river. There was also the murmur of the real river. And the Great Blue Heron in the reeds. And the Red-tailed hawk perched on the alder branch. And, best of all, Yellow-rumped Warblers in the oceanspray and blackberry bushes along the path. I'm making it sound very romantic, when really it was a trial in classroom management without the classroom (thus, wildlife management?). These kids were clearly not used to learning without walls. But after threats to send the rowdiest of the boys back inside, they all piped down. It seemed they really wanted to be there.

My pedagogical goal was to help my students expand their ability to see—to use all their senses to take in their environment—then turn the whole thing into a lovely writing exercise. I thought this a pretty straightforward goal. The problem was I couldn't get them to close their eyes. They kept looking up, around, down, obviously feasting on what they saw. Their inability to focus was based on the fact that not one of them had ever been to this wetland before and they wanted to see what was around them. Most had attended this school since kindergarten, which meant that they had spent ten years of school days within a few hundred meters of this very wetland, but never knew it was there. I was astonished. Now if *I* had been the science teacher—ha!—I would have started our lessons with a weekly walk down to the wetland. We would have created a bio-inventory of the ecosystem and tracked the seasonal shifts in species populations and water levels. We would have created our own field guides and illustrated them with the animals, birds, and plants we saw, touched, and smelled. Oh, it would have been so educational. If only, if only!

Actually, if I had it to do over I would have taken the classes I *did* teach down to that wetland more than just once. I would have taught them the art of observation and keeping quiet. I would have read aloud—while sitting on a stump, to the backdrop of bird song!—from Aldo Leopold and Annie Dillard.

I would have offered them their own place as a window into wonder.

7

Mindful Meals

*Eaters must understand that eating takes place inescapably in
the world, that it is inescapably an agricultural act, and that
how we eat determines, to a considerable extent,
how the world is used.*

WENDELL BERRY

IN OUR MIND'S EYE the A Rocha enterprise was meant to be about
conservation and education, anchored in community. Food was
the stuff that fueled these enterprises; we didn't intend it to be an
enterprise in and of itself. But landing at our first environmental center and looking out the farmhouse's bay window onto the
rich brown soil of the half-acre garden plot, we suddenly began
dreaming of growing enough food to feed guests and interns. How
romantic and sustainable—the zero-mile diet! We fantasized of
roasted beets sprinkled with goat cheese and fresh tomato and

basil salads. The more we fantasized the more we realized that, like everything else, it's all connected. The means is always the end, and if we wanted to take environmental stewardship seriously, then we'd have to be consistent in what we ate at the Center.

We moved in August, not the best month for planting, but Markku found some swiss chard seedlings at a nearby nursery and I planted them in one humble row—a sentinel against the half-acre of dirt. That row produced copious amounts of leaves, which we ate like lettuce (because we couldn't think how else to consume them) until Christmas. So much for gourmet! The next spring we planted two scraggly rows of English peas and three rows of lettuce which bolted before we could eat a quarter of it. We had sown all our seeds at once, without a plan for subsequent harvests. Duh. A row of corn replaced the Swiss chard sentinel on the edge of the plot and produced a whopping three edible ears. Finally, we planted a small colony of artichoke plants, which produced one crop of eight slightly anemic bulbs of fruit, which we harvested and ate at a community meal with a mother and son who were backpacking from Alaska to California, and whom we discovered one morning asleep in their tent, pitched for the night next to our pond. Most of that first summer we just grew weeds.

THE ARTICHOKE: WEED OR DELICACY?

Needless to say, if the Center were to produce a decent amount of edible food we would need a real farmer. That farmer arrived in the form of Paul Neufeld. From solid Manitoban Mennonite stock, he has been an indescribable gift to the A Rocha community. Quiet and calm, he has ably accommodated a revolving door of interns and volunteers who have come over the years to get their hands dirty while learning the art of organic gardening. Under his care A Rocha has not only fed thousands of volunteers and interns at our Center, but has also developed a thriving Community Shared Agriculture (CSA) project. We chose the CSA model rather than a roadside stand because this weekly vegetable share program connects families directly with a farmer and thus to their food. The participants pay upfront for a season of produce, thereby joining with the farmer in the ups (bumper cucumber harvests) and downs (unforeseen tomato blight) of farm life. Unlike an urban organic box program where participants select items from a long list of options, CSA shareholders receive whatever is currently being harvested. The CSA movement is relatively young, starting in the 1960s simultaneously in Europe and Japan and coming on the North American scene as late as the 1980s. While the largest CSAs can have thousands of participants ("Farm Fresh to You" in Capay Valley, California boasts four thousand families), most are humble affairs with under one hundred "shareholders."

The thing that strikes me as funny (and tragic) is how many people look out on our couple acres of garden and ask, "Oh, so is this CSA how you support the work of A Rocha?" If they mean philosophically and programmatically support A Rocha's work, then, yes, it most certainly does. But if they mean (which they often do), does the sale of CSA shares financially support the work of A Rocha? Then the answer is, no. Somehow, despite having seen all those FarmAid concerts, people still believe the average farmer can make a living farming. The sad reality is that whereas one hundred years ago a farmer received forty cents of every dollar spent on food, today less than seven cents of every "food dollar" trickles back to the farmer. The rest is absorbed by one of a handful of agribusiness monoliths that turn kernels of corn into thousands of wonderful and wacky processed and packaged food items.

So, no, the revenues from our CSA—a CSA which produces over ten thousand pounds of veggies a season and feeds over 150 people a week!—make up just half of Paul's part-time salary. The other half he raises from like-minded friends, church, and family members, who understand his vocation as Christian ministry. But we didn't enter into the CSA experiment because we thought it'd keep A Rocha financially afloat. And Paul didn't become a farmer because he wanted to get rich. As I said, our foray into agriculture wasn't really premeditated. We just happened to find ourselves at an Environmental Center that came with five acres of garden and pasture land, and it seemed a shame not to cultivate it. Because of Paul's willingness and expertise, A Rocha fell into farming, making sustainable agriculture the third leg, along with conservation and education, on which the A Rocha program stool rests.

THE ORGANIC DEBATE

Because we are now in the food game, people are constantly trying to get us to weigh in on the organic versus conventional food debate. "Is organic really better?" they want to know. When asked, we try to defer to our resident expert, Paul, but he's usually out in the field up to his elbows in dirt and it seems counterproductive to pull him away from *planting* vegetables to *talk* about vegetables. So we attempt an answer. Our first response is, "Better, how?" Nutritionally? Economically? Environmentally? It's interesting, but nearly to a person, if it's a member of the older (fifty years and above) set asking, they want to know if it's better nutritionally. The answer is complicated and hard to answer with clear scientific backing. It is true that conventionally grown produce is doused with pesticides and herbicides that have been shown, when consumed in high levels, to act as neurotoxins, endocrine disruptors, and carcinogens, but the amount of these toxins one actually ingests in a given pear or potato might still be harmless. Might. That one's still up in the air.

Toxicity aside, what about nutritional value? Again, as Michael Pollan points out, it's tough to say with empirical certainty since so many variables effect a vegetable's nutritional quality (things like geography, freshness, genetics, soils, etc.). What is becoming more qualifiable is the higher levels of micronutrients and polyphenols present in organically grown plants. Polyphenols are chemical metabolites that help plants metabolize nutrients and are found especially in the skins of fruits. A study by researchers at the University of California-Davis which looked at vitamin and polyphenol levels in organic and conventionally grown foods has shed new light on the benefit of organically grown produce. The organic fruits and veggies consistently had higher levels of vitamin C and a wide range of polyphenols, which have antioxidant and antimicrobial properties. Why were levels higher? The researchers theorize that without the benefit of pesticides and herbicides the plants must defend themselves naturally (via polyphenols) against pests or succumb, making for stronger, healthier plants. That's one theory. The other is that by drastically simplifying the soil with chemical fertilizers and no compost or rotational crops, plants no longer have the ingredients to produce these compounds. Other studies have shown similar patterns. So, yes, organically grown food is most likely more nutritional. But, frankly, I must add that this is not the primary reason we grow organic veggies at A Rocha. We are quite conscious of the fact that eating only "organic" can be quite self-serving, especially if the organic fruit or vegetable in question has traveled hundreds of miles to one's plate. After all, doesn't shelling out two dollars for an organic apple from New Zealand seem a bit outrageous when the rest of the world starves for a bit of vitamin C?

Finally, there's the environmental angle. No petro-chemicals (in the forms of fertilizers, pesticides, and herbicides) equals more environmental, right? Yes . . . and no. Growing plants and animals using organic methods does mean less soil erosion, less nitrogen run-off and no toxic pesticides, herbicides, and growth hormones in the watershed—all huge factors in sustaining healthy ecosystems. So, yes, organic is tremendously better for the health of the planet. Hurray. To celebrate that bit of happy news I just snuck one of my daughter's EnviroKidz Organic Crispy Rice bars, six to a box and conveniently individually wrapped. The package boasts that this little bit of crunchy chocolate goodness is gluten-free, low in sodium, has zero grams of trans fat and contains nothing artificial.

And best of all one percent of the proceeds from the purchase will be donated to a worthy conservation organization. Hurray again.

But, as my Crispy Rice Bar attests, "organic" ain't what it used to be. We now have the oxymoronical beast known as "industrial organic" which operates in the agri-business mode, only without all the petro-chemicals. It's a good news/bad news scenario. On the one hand these companies and their farms aren't sterilizing soil or polluting streams, a benefit that cannot be overemphasized. But they still use around eight calories of fossil fuel energy to deliver one calorie of food energy to my table. While the soil might be happier, the air gets just as polluted, tons of carbon is released into the atmosphere, and the whole model rests on an ever-dwindling supply of cheap oil.

HOMEGROWN

And so we arrive at the "Eat Local" craze, a fad born both out of an environmental ethic as well as personal concern over the safety of food from industrial farms and feedlots where a single E. coli outbreak at a single farm can infect thousands of people across thousands of miles. Just when you thought those dreadlocked vegans had the moral upper ground in the food ethics wars, along come the above repute locavores. These folk religiously track food miles so as to avoid being tainted by a peach or pear that might have been grown outside their own hundred-mile radius. Actually, I don't know why I'm making fun of them—in my best moments I want to join them! I applaud my locavore friends living in a community house in inner-city Vancouver. In an effort to encourage one another to use up every last ingredient in their weekly A Rocha CSA share they instituted a little competition. Every meal is evaluated according to a point system calibrated to food miles and organics. A locally grown spinach, garlic, and tomato frittata made from free-range eggs and augmented with homemade salsa, for example, will earn you approximately ten points. Harvest those ingredients from your own backyard garden and you've doubled your points. Open a jar for that salsa and lose a point. Open two jars (for the pre-crushed garlic!?) and lose two points. You get the idea. The competition lasts throughout the growing season and has become the cornerstone of their communal culinary life, resulting in great fun for both chefs and eaters.

While we have never gone so far as a point system at the A Rocha Center, we do have our scruples and no-go areas—things like feedlot beef, soda pop, and processed snack food. And though we are situated in British Columbia, we do eat wheat from Saskatchewan and the occasional fruit from California in the winter. But where possible, we eat locally produced produce, which is especially easy in the summer and fall when our gardens are burgeoning. In so doing we've discovered the joys of eating in season. This has given rise to theme meals. One volunteer day, for example, everything we served contained zucchini—soup, salad, bread, and even the desert in the form of chocolate zucchini cake. Another volunteer day was pumpkin day. Still another, beet day. While the challenge of working a root vegetable into a palatable desert can be quite the culinary thrill, I must admit adhering to a locavore diet has its struggles. By March we are all sick and tired of kale, about the only thing that will grow through the winter in our garden.

The main thing is, we try to eat real food from a bit lower on the food chain. It's our meager stand of solidarity with our brothers and sisters in the two-thirds world for whom a locally grown, mostly vegetarian diet is the norm. Therefore, the A Rocha pantry is full of beans of every sort, as well as rice, millet, wheat, spelt, and canned tomatoes.

Interns and volunteers must adapt. At least in public. Truth be told, I've wandered into the girls' dorm room and gotten a peek in the closet, finding it stocked with bottles of Coke and bags of chips, to which I turned a kindly blind eye. Life's a journey after all—a journey I'm still on, as my own private cupboards testify.

But most interns take our food agenda in stride, or at least they try to. In the beginning lentils are novel, and they feel noble eating like so many in the two-thirds world. But after a week or two this wears off and there is a clamoring for meat—big chunks of it. In this case I'm reminded of our intern Martin Lings (he of the burnt shrew fame). I was in charge of the food during our first nine months at the first environmental center until Celeste, whose name connotes the quality of her cooking, arrived and took over for that first full summer. Now, I'm not a terrible cook, but I was run a bit off my feet in those early days and my cooking suffered as a result. I recall one particular day when I had morphed left-over lentils into their third incarnation. This simple little act of efficiency caused Martin, normally the height of English civility, to positively lose it. The scene went something like this:

Me: *Sauntering to the table with a child on my hip and casserole dish in hand—the very picture of female domesticity.* "Dinner's served!"

Martin: *Staring hungrily from the table.* "Smells good, what's for tea (read: supper)?"

Me: *Coyly.* "Oh, just a little lentil thing I refashioned."

Martin: *Face falling, eyeing the casserole dish suspiciously.* "Huh?"

Me: *Smiling a bit too brightly. No comment as I lift the casserole lid.*

Martin: *Wailing.* "Nooooooo, not Lentil Goo again!"

So, of course, I assigned him to cook the next dinner. He made chicken and avocados in white sauce. I'm pretty sure the chicken was from an industrial farm and the avocados were from Mexico, but it was delicious. And since at A Rocha relationships always take precedence over moral jockeying, I told him so.

But Martin wasn't always so successful in the kitchen. His most spectacular failure came when he got a hankering for a taste of home and announced he was going to whip up a batch of Cornish Pasties. None of us had any idea what these were, but they sounded promisingly bready and flakey so we gave him the thumbs up and left him to it. He labored away in the kitchen for a half an hour and then got stymied by the recipe's instructions to "cut in butter to pea-sized crumbs." Being a scientist he took the recipe at its most literal and proceeded accordingly, though with increasing apprehension. About twenty minutes later he hailed Tiina from the office for a bit of womanly perspective. She took one look at his creation, clapped her hand to her mouth and ran to gather the other office workers, who "had to get a look at this!" Poor Martin had spent the previous twenty minutes smearing a pound of butter to an exact one-eighth-inch thickness onto the largest cookie sheet in the kitchen. He then proceeded to painstakingly cut that butter into one-eighth-inch cubes until he had about a thousand pea-sized "crumbs" of butter. What flummoxed him—and sent him in search of Tiina—was what to do with the butter next. How on earth were all those little cubes of butter to become Cornish Pasties? After recovering from hysterical laughter, Tiina helped him corral the butter into a bowl, added flour and instructed him in the wonders of a pastry cutter. It proved to be an important lesson in the value of mentoring (and, for that matter, syntax—it makes all the difference in the world upon which side of "butter" that little "in" falls).

FOOD ART

Without question the apex of A Rocha's early culinary history occurred during Brian Marek's four-year tenure as Center cook. In truth, he was more of an "artist in residence" than strictly a cook. In true truth, he was more of a philosopher/artist in residence, peppering his meals and cooking lessons with musings on Heidegger and metaphysics. Many an intern would later reflect that though they had come to learn about conservation or environmental education it was their time in the kitchen with Brian that made the biggest impact in their lives—there they had learned not only how to cook a mean curried squash soup, but also how to philosophically connect the everydayness of eating to the larger picture of their most cherished environmental values.

But lest you think Brian was all cerebral idealism, let it be known that he knew how to party. I think the technical culinary term is feast. In this vein he instituted regularly occurring theme feasts. He'd put on a Putamayo World Music CD appropriate to the region (i.e., "Italian Cafe," "French Playground," "Brazilian Lounge," etc.) and cook up a storm. The verdict is out on his most successful meal, but my personal favorite was an Italian feast he prepared for A Rocha International's Board of Trustees. The centerpiece of the meal was a dish called Timpano—a dish made famous in the movie *Big Night* and which contains, according to the movie's main character, "all the good things in life." A good portion of the movie involves the making and eating of Timpano and a strong contingent of staff and interns spent a good portion of an entire day preparing it in A Rocha's kitchen. Zitti pasta was hand rolled on a floured table, homemade red sauce simmered on the stove, ground beef and spices were pressed into tidy balls. These ingredients were layered along with peas, chicken, mozzarella, and hard-boiled eggs inside a pastry crust baked in a giant glass bowl, giving it the shape of a drum (hence the name Timpano). After an hour in the oven, the Timpanos (or Timpani?) were set on platters before our expectant guests. The defining moment came when Brian sliced into the first drum revealing a succulent strata of cheeses, meats, and sauce. The result was so magnificent that we all applauded—just like they did in the movie.

Did I mention we dressed up for theme nights? Sombreros on Mexican food night, nun's habits on the *Sound of Music*/Austrian food night and, of course, plaid blankets pinned over our jeans for make-shift kilts for Robbie Burns night. For this latter feast Brian set his cooking utensils and locavore values aside and purchased a bona fide haggis from a shop called the Celtic Treasure Chest

(purveyors of fair isle sweaters, harp and fiddle CDs, and, of course, haggis). With all the time he saved not having to stuff sheep's intestines with oatmeal, he committed to memory Robert Burns' immortal poem, "Ode to the Haggis," which he recited in full Scottish brogue to our great delight. You just gotta love a poem with lines like "Trenching your gushing entrails bright." I can't say we loved the actual haggis quite as much. Personally, I prefer my oatmeal seasoned with brown sugar rather than tripe. Aida, the one year-old daughter of our Center Directors Jay and Milissa, however, was crazy about it. While the rest of us nibbled politely at our portions, Aida dug in with gusto. Unfortunately, the large amount of lard mixed in with those oats produced quite the tummy ache for little Aida later, and she was up half the night in intestinal agony. Her suffering was in turn felt by Brian, since her bedroom was on the other side of the wall from his own. As he lay in bed in the wee hours of the night with the sound of Aida's moaning in his ears, I'm sure he teased out some metaphysical treatise on the deterministic theory of causality and how haggis fit into the mix.

STRIKING A BALANCE

So, we feasted. Feasting came easy to us. If there's one thing we know how to do in North America it's feast. From the point of view of caloric intake, we feast every day, thanks to the way the food industry has smuggled corn syrup into everything from tea—yes, tea!—to turkey popovers. What we don't know how to do is fast. At A Rocha, the ballast for all this societal feasting is the Center's noontime meal, when up to forty of us gather around a common table. The meal is often monastic in its simplicity—hearty bread and a bowl of savory soup is the norm. The Mennonite Central Committee (MCC) cookbooks have become our bible for these meals. They include simple recipes, with simple seasonal ingredients, and simple steps. They are perfect for your nineteen-year-old British intern whose cooking exploits have yet to soar beyond soft-boiled eggs and toast.

The adjustment to simplicity in eating has come more naturally to some of us than others. For those who've found the transition difficult, the rub usually comes from their own cultural biases. Take Markku: a Finn raised in Nepal, two cultures that highly value hospitality, the hallmark of which is providing copious amounts of food for one's guests. When we first started running the Center, a visitor would arrive and Markku wanted to pull out the red carpet—and I wasn't far behind. For breakfasts, we'd run out and buy fancy muesli cereal in attractive boxes, accompanied by artisan bread with orange juice. But our housemate, and A Rocha's accountant, Jessica said "no." Dear, idealistic Jessica, who spent four years training us in the ways of simplicity and sustainability, said no. Staying at A Rocha's Environmental Center was not meant to be a holiday, but an education. Give them oats, bought in bulk, stored in an old pickle jar, and let them make porridge. And no orange juice, either! Let them drink tea. To a Finn this was tantamount to tossing a guest a piece of moldy bread!

Fortunately, exceptions were made for specials guests—those who'd traveled far or who were just visiting for a day or who were members of A Rocha's Board of Directors. Unfortunately, sometimes these sort of special guests, deserving special sorts and quantities of food, arrived unannounced. Now, visitors arrive unannounced all the time at A Rocha, and usually they are invited to stay for lunch, and usually there's plenty to go around. But one day the cook in charge (not Brian, in case you're wondering) had made very fancy Japanese pancake somethings which evidently took a lot of work. They took so much work that the cook of the day decided to go for quality rather than quantity. It just so happened that three Board members showed up just as we were sitting to eat. (In fairness to the cook these guests were unexpected only to her—we knew they were coming but forgot to tell her.) Everyone was served one meagre little pancake thing and that was it—not even a sprig of parsley to disguise the austerity. It was the loneliest looking piece of food I'd ever seen.

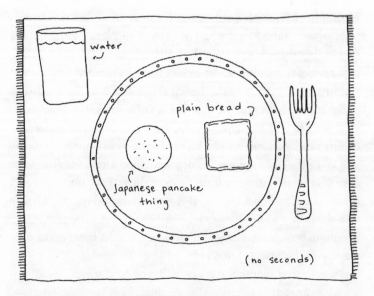

I stole a glance at Markku, who, due to his Finnish sensibilities, was practically apoplectic with suppressed anxiety. Someone scurried into the kitchen and found a wayward loaf of sandwich bread to augment the pancakes. So then the meal consisted of one small pancake, one slice of square brown bread, and water.

In hindsight, this austere meal was probably a good move, spurring our board members into more active fundraising to bolster our obviously pathetic food budget.

THE LADEN TABLE

In contrast to the Great Pancake Fiasco, the predominant theme overarching all the farming and eating at A Rocha's Center has been one of abundance. Weekly CSA baskets (actually, big Rubbermaid blue tubs) overflow with up to twenty different selections of produce, from potatoes to spinach to rutabagas. The bounty is so copious that most CSA members split their share with another household since they find it impossible to make it through all those veggies in one week. Reflecting on this theme of abundance, our farmer Paul summed it up well in one of his regular CSA newsletters: "Such abundance is a gift, and makes possible other gifts: healthy bodies and minds nourished by good food; the raw materials for hospitality; the opportunity for generosity; the necessity of creativity in the kitchen (what to do with kohlrabi?); and the reminder that all of this comes from the hand of our generous Creator!"

At A Rocha centers we don't have a chapel, we have a table. The meal is a place of community, fellowship, and invitation. Conversations range from favorite films to theology to birds sighted on the morning bird walk to the number of eggs laid by the hens that morning to more personal family histories. The table is a safe place, a neutral ground for dialogue, knowing, and communion. Is it any wonder that the New Testament is full of accounts of Jesus eating meals with people (and with the most unlikely people)? Is it any wonder that Jesus chose a meal to commemorate the abundance of his love?

8

Rescuing the Ox from the Well

*I care not for a man's religion if his dog and cat are not the
better for it.*

Abraham Lincoln

Once you move to a farm you need farm animals. So thought
our friend Bob, now affectionately known as Bob the Cow Guy. A
horticulturist and owner of one of the first native plant nurseries in
the Vancouver area, he stopped in about a week after we arrived to
check out the place. After a lap around the property he said, "You
need some animals."

Markku laughed off the comment, saying that A Rocha didn't
even own the property yet and that conservation and education *not*
animal husbandry were our first concerns. That said, yes, someday,
perhaps, we might get a cow or a sheep or at least a rabbit.

Bob shook his head in an I-know-something-you-don't-know kind of way and said no more—for the moment. He called a week later.

"I've got your cows," were the first words out of his mouth.

"Our cows?" replied Markku.

"Six or seven, maybe a couple more," said Bob.

Now Markku was worried. He emphasized again that A Rocha didn't own the property. We were still trying to drum up the $250,000 for the down payment. Besides that, we only had four acres of pasture which were extremely soggy in the winter. Two, or at most four, cows would be the eventual max. Finally, we didn't know the first thing about raising cows.

"Well," said Bob. "My friend is going through a divorce and needs to get rid of them. He's feeling really desperate and, well, I've already paid for them." Cue the violins.

"And," he added. "They're Highland Cows. You know, those cute Scottish ones."

Markku's resistance crumbled. He told Bob we'd ask the Leitzes about it. They turned out to have a penchant for interesting animals, having kept a menagerie of exotic creatures, including emus and llamas, on the property over their thirty-year ownership. I can't recall if they or we had any plan for what we'd do with these shaggy ruminants should the deal with A Rocha fall through. Take them to our house in White Rock with the postage stamp yard? Advertise them on Craigslist? Without a thought to contingency plans, Markku told Bob we would take four. He'd just have to find homes for the others.

"Right," said Bob. "No problem."

He arrived a few days later towing a horse trailer behind his diesel truck. Six shaggy cows emerged from the trailer. He was right, they were very cute, but there were two too many. We had agreed on four.

We protested.

He countered. What was he going to do, take the extras to the SPCA? (Actually, he could have, but none of us realized this at the time.)

So we said, oh alright, gave the cows some hay, and tried to wrap our minds around animal husbandry.

Two days later we got a call from Bob.

"Where are you?" asked Markku.

"In your driveway," said Bob.

Markku rushed out. Two more cows stood timidly in the field. (Or was that Bob who stood so timidly?)

"That's it," said Markku. "No more cows!"

Bob looked thoroughly chastened. "Of course, of course," he mumbled.

Another two days passed. We were eating breakfast when we heard the unmistakable rumble of a diesel engine.

"That sounds like Bob's truck," said Markku, looking at me in alarm. He threw down his spoon and dashed from the kitchen. Bob was just leaving, having snuck two more cows into the pasture.

FACTORY FARMING WILBUR

Thus began a small-scale adventure in cattle rearing and eating. Eating these cows and their offspring—which Bob and the A Rocha community have, one by one, over the span of seven years—got us thinking about the myriad issues surrounding meat farming: issues ranging from the well-being of the animals themselves to the well-being of those who eat them to the well-being of the planet that supports them. The issue of human health has become headline news in recent years, with outbreaks E. coli in factory farms resulting in illness and even deaths among consumers. This in turn has opened the door for a more critical look at the inhumane conditions of many factory farms and feedlots. Bestselling books like *Fast Food Nation* and *Omnivore's Dilemma,* as well as undercover videos taken by the Humane Society and other animal rights groups at farms as well as slaughter facilities, have gone a long way in bringing the plight of factory farm animals to light.

The biggest contributor to ill-treatment, of course, is overcrowding, which gives rise to all sorts of neurotic behaviors in the animals. Take pigs, for example. Normally sociable and intelligent creatures, in more wild settings they live in complex matriarchal family groups and even care for one another's young. Pigs are also, despite the fact that their name has become synonymous with slovenliness, clean animals, building their nests on hillsides so that their own waste runs down and away from their living quarters. But wean them at just three weeks of age, pack them by the thousands in musty, dimly lit barns, and all their sociability flies out the window. They become stressed out and aggressive and take to tail biting (not their own, of course, but the pig's nearest them). The solution: cut off their tails. The benefit of a tailless pig is primarily for the farmer, however, because his real problem is not the tail biting, but his pigs' general state of lethargy. Evidently, as Michael Pollan discovered on his visit to a factory pig farm, a depressed pig will do nothing to defend its derrière, which when bit repeatedly will become infected, resulting in a sick pig. But a docked tail is a sensitive tail, and when bit, the pig in question will yelp and scamper out of harm's way. Problem solved.

Chickens don't have it much better. Ninety-five percent of all eggs bought in the U.S. come from caged hens. Confining chickens to small quarters allows farmers to produce eggs at a staggering rate. A single "farm" can produce over two million eggs a day from three million hens. These hens live in wire battery cages (now banned in the EU) with just sixty-seven square inches of "personal space" per bird—not enough to even flap their wings. If left to themselves in such conditions the chickens would peck each other to death and so are de-beaked. To add insult to injury, toes are also removed to ensure that their feet don't grow into the mesh of the cages.

How did these animals come to be treated so abysmally? The answer is scale. Care for fifty pigs or two hundred chickens on the family farm, and you're in the field of animal husbandry. Care for 5,000 pigs or 200,000 chickens, and you're in the field of industry. And industry plays by a whole different set of rules, because the industrial playbook is written with an eye toward efficiency and profit rather than the thoughtful care of individual animals.

Bernard Rollin, professor of Philosophy, Physiology, and Animal Sciences at Colorado State University, unpacks this shift from husbandry to industry. Because in most husbandry models farmers worked on a small scale, they couldn't afford to lose animals to disease or ill-treatment, nor could they afford a battery of antibiotics or vitamin supplements. Furthermore, because animals in distress are not as reproductive and robust as well-cared-for animals, a symbiosis developed whereby the animal and farmer both benefited—the animal with a happy life and the farmer with a healthy "product." And because in the olden days consumers knew where their meat came from, they were sure to buy from those farmers with the reputation for the best beef or pork or poultry.

CHECKING WITH SCRIPTURE

Where does the Bible land on the issue of animal welfare? Well, if the biblical ethic toward creation is one of *caring* and *keeping*, such ill-treatment of animals found in much of industrialized meat production warrants our consideration. Not only do both the Hebrew and Christian scriptures provide a theological foundation for earthkeeping in general, they are also full of specific commands about treating animals well. Here's a short sampling of paraphrased verses:

- A righteous person cares for the needs of his animals. (Prov 12:10)

- Help raise to its feet an animal that is down even if it belongs to your enemy. (Exod 23:12 and Deut 22:4)

- Rescue a son *or an ox* that has fallen into a well, even on the Sabbath. (Luke 14:5)

- Don't muzzle an ox while it's threshing (because doing so would prohibit the animal from enjoying a reward while working). (Deut 25:4)

- Don't yoke an ox and ass together (because of the hardship it would cause for the weaker animal). (Deut 22:10)

True, you won't find any verses saying, "Thou shalt not let thy cows stand knee-deep in manure at thy cattle feedlot," but that's only because the biblical writers couldn't imagine or predict such a thing. What they could imagine and what they advocated for was shalom—a state of well-being characterized by harmony, not only between humanity and God, but also between humanity and the rest of creation. Shalom occurs when people treat each other and the whole earth with thoughtfulness.

ANIMAL HUSBANDRY 101

Thus we chose to avoid industrially farmed meat at the A Rocha Center. We've learned a fair bit about the issues, but there's always more to learn about the animals themselves. The cow learning curve was certainly steep, illustrated by a simple little mistake we made with one of our Highlands back in those early days.

Her name was Shaggy, and she was big and blond. After a few weeks on the farm we noticed that she walked with a pronounced swagger that all of us previously pregnant types immediately recognized. In consideration of her condition we put her in a special corral to keep an eye on her while she gestated. Soon school kids on field trips were peering at her from across the fence as we said, proud as grandparents, "Look at our pregnant cow!"

maternal eyes

friendly disposition

VERY shaggy

"SHAGGY"
THE HIGHLAND COW

Then a neighbor who runs a cattle feedlot (a very small-scale, friendly sort of feedlot) stopped by. After inspecting our herd with the bemused air of an expert dealing with amateurs, he asked about the cow quarantined to the corral.

"She's pregnant," explained Markku.

"Pregnant, eh?" said Vern, the feedlot man, scratching his chin.

"Yeah, do you have any advice? Anything we should know?"

Vern scratched his chin some more and bent down to inspect the under regions of Shaggy. He stood slowly like he had a sore back. A wry smile spread across his face.

"First thing you should know," he said. "That ain't no cow."

Lesson one in animal husbandry: get your genders right. Turns out the swagger was due to a sore foot.

Lesson two: get your gates right. We learned this lesson one morning as I stumbled bleary-eyed from bed towards the bathroom and happened to glance out the window. I stood paralyzed for a good ten seconds, then rubbed my eyes just like they do in the comic books. There in the field opposite our house stood our ten cows, facing due west toward the adjacent field. There in the adjacent field, facing due east toward our ten cows, were *fifty* large and meaty looking bovines, strangers all.

I yelled for Markku, who was still asleep. I didn't go get him because I didn't trust the mirage of visitor cows to still be there when I got back. I called again with more urgency. The two herds continued their silent cross-fence contemplation, serene and steaming in the morning sun. Finally Markku emerged, and I pointed out the window.

One encounters such purely surreal moments only a few times in one's life and this one was magnificent. Time slowed and wonder reigned as we both stood transfixed in our bewilderment. And a profound communion, born out of a shared encounter with mystery, settled upon us. Never mind that this mystery was merely the banal question, "Where in the world did all those cows come from!?" It's hardly a metaphysical conundrum, and yet we savored every incongruous and sublime second of it.

Of course, the mystery faded pretty quickly as we surmised that our new borders could have come from only one place—the feedlot down the street. Now it was Markku's turn to play the know-it-all. He called Vern and asked if he was missing anything. Nope, he didn't think so. Markku told him to go check his barns and then call back. The phone rang and a sheepish voice confessed that the previous night's truckload of cattle had escaped. Evidently they had meandered down 172nd Street into suburbia, saw our cows in a pleasant pasture, and herded in for an autumnal tête à tête. Actually, a few never made it into our field. One ended up a couple of kilometers away on the shores of the Pacific Ocean, providing more than one beach-goer with a sublime moment of incongruity as they contemplated the Black Angus ambling through the intertidal zone.

EATING SHAGGY

They say you should never name an animal you plan on eating. Perhaps, but I'll say one thing: when you know it's Shaggy on your plate, it sure adds authenticity to your pre-meal prayer. Firsthand knowledge of your dinner's name brings you face to face with the fact that everything that feeds us—from a beef steak to a beefsteak tomato—has to die to give us life. As Gary Synder so ably puts it, "If we do eat meat, it is the life, the bounce, the swish, of a great alert being with keen ears and lovely eyes, with four square feet and a huge beating heart that we eat, let us not deceive ourselves."

Rick Faw taught us a lot in this regard. Rick, who serves as A Rocha's Education Director, came with his family to live at the Field Study Center the spring after we arrived. One of the first tasks we bequeathed to him was the care of the cows, a task he gladly accepted, being a closet cow whisperer and all-around animal lover. The image that stays with me from those early days is of Rick, baby Jared on his back and a farm cat at his heels, pushing a wheelbarrow towering with hay through the sodden grass to the pasture. He'd deftly launch the bales over the fence and into the cows' troughs, pet their foreheads while they munched, and then go on with his other farm chores. This was his morning routine.

In the late afternoons, while Jared napped, Rick returned to the fields to brush the cows. I think he really wanted a dog, or any more sentient sort of pet, but since he had cows, he poured all his pent-up pet affection into them. He'd stand out there, in the cold, in his 1980s bright blue ski jacket, and brush those cows down as if they were Thoroughbreds and tomorrow was the Kentucky Derby. Markku and I watched all this from our kitchen window and, I must admit, wondered if Rick was making the best use of his time. Surely he could be writing a fundraising letter or planning a talk or following up with potential interns. There was just so much to be done.

Our attitude just goes to show our lack of groundedness. Brushing the cows, by Rick's own admission, served no practical function. Highland cattle on the moors of Scotland never get their coats brushed and they survive just fine. A few burrs and tangles in no way mitigates their enjoyment of sun, grass, and stars. But then Rick wasn't really concerned with burrs and tangles; the brushing was a way of de-stressing for Rick (and probably for the cows as well). In this way it was both an act of contemplation and even, dare I say, of fellowship. Given his bonding with these beasts you'd think Rick would have been the first of us to go vegetarian (I alone of all the A Rocha staff hold that distinction). But no, he ate the stews and roasts just like everyone else. He did admit, however, that he felt a measure of sadness when eating our cows, but for him this was a good thing, for in his sadness lay the seeds of gratitude.

My personal litmus test for what meat my family eats turns on two questions. First: did the animal in question live a happy and normal life? Did it eat grass if it was naturally a grass eater, flap its wings if it was naturally a wing flapper, and so on. Second: would I be okay with raising and then killing said animal myself? Don't get me wrong, I'm not saying I have actually killed any of the meat (what little meat there is) on my family's table. What I am saying is that it's really important to acknowledge that that nugget on my plate was once a clucking, roosting chicken and that hot dog in its bun was once a grunting, snuffling pig. Making these sorts of connections helps me live more thankfully and *care*fully. Making these connections helps me to make food choices within the rubric of my moral convictions. If we concede the "animality" of the meat we eat, then we need to be reconciled to the fact that eating meat, by necessity, involves killing, blood, death.

This only-eat-it-if-you're-willing-to-kill-it position is also the stance taken by Loren and Mary Ruth Wilkinson, professors at Regent College in Vancouver and teachers of a class on food and theology. Their week-long food course, held on their cooperative sheep farm on Galiano Island, is full of theological readings, discussion, and lots of very good food. The high point of the week is a meal—a Supper of the Lamb—which encapsulates all the learning of the class. The main course and lamb in question is as local as local gets, having frolicked in the fields outside the Wilkinson's window all its short life. The meal is held on a Friday evening and on the Wednesday previous, everyone gathers outside the sheep barn. A professional lamb slaughterer from Saturna Island is in attendance and does the actual killing, very humanely, with a bolt gun. Everyone, including the vegetarians, is encouraged to participate in the rest of the process of skinning and gutting. Often, ironically, it is a vegetarian who takes a lead role in the whole drama.

When I asked about the lamb's slaughter, Mary Ruth reflected on her own experience: "It is actually a reverent honoring—a bringing together of the ecological reality and the biblical principle of how we live. For me the lamb's whole body is so startling a revelation of my own body, of my own innards, that I feel a great kinship and thankfulness not only for the lamb, but, by extension, for the life of creation that is given to and for me."

Of course, the Christian symbolism inherent in a "Supper of the Lamb" was not lost on anyone. Having met the innocent, short-lived lamb for themselves, and then participated in its slaughter, the connotations of sacrifice were forefront in everyone's mind.

MR. DARCY MEETS HIS MAKER

I readily admit a city squeamishness towards the slaughter of animals—hence my leaning toward vegetarianism. I can handle meat neatly cut and shrink-wrapped in plastic, but the transition from frolicking in the field to fried on the plate makes me queasy, even if the animal in question seems deserving of his fried fate. In this regard I'm thinking of one animal in particular—one rooster in particular: Mr. Darcy. Named after the guy who bequeathed him to us, he displayed the supremely superior air of the *Pride and Prejudice* character and thus got saddled with the "Mr." prefix.

But it wasn't his haughtiness that made him so deserving of death. Such an attribute is to be expected in one possessing such splendid plumage. Rather, it was his viciousness that sent him to death row—his viciousness toward *my* child. You see, Maya, like all farm-raised four-year-olds, had a fascination with collecting eggs. She'd trot into the coop and fill her basket with brown, green, and white eggs, heedless of the proud roosters who strutted along the fence behind her. But all that changed one spring day. On that particular morning I handed Maya her little egg basket and blithely sent her into the chicken coop, right into Mr. Darcy's domain. As she made her way to the back of the coop, he came charging—wings flapping, talons outstretched in his most savage cockfighting impersonation. Maya screamed bloody murder; Mr. Darcy flapped and scratched (Maya's face!) and I stood paralyzed in horror. Fortunately, not for long. Arms flailing, I rushed at the offending bird and booted him across the coop with a swift soccer kick (he was surprisingly solid), snatched Maya off the ground, and made a dash for safety.

After Mr. Darcy had shown his true colors, only brave Brian, our philosopher-cook, collected the eggs, armed with a garbage can lid, which he used as a shield. Brian was also the one who scheduled Mr. Darcy's slaughter a few weeks later. Tiina, our office manager, had a farm savvy friend from church who agreed to come and kill the bully rooster and a few of his brothers. The slaughtering, plucking, and cooking took a good part of the day. Suburban wimp that I am, I used the excuse of not wanting to traumatize the children and whisked them off to a playdate during the actual execution. By the accounts of Brian and Tiina all the birds did the traditional headless chicken dance as their life's electricity exited their nervous systems. Then came the scalding and the plucking.

I finally joined everyone in the kitchen for the gutting and dressing. Brian plunked a big-breasted, puckered-skinned bird on the counter in front of me. I swallowed hard and decided the best way to attack my meat queasiness was to really go on the attack. I stabbed at the bird's abdomen and with a swift slice upward opened its innards to plain view.

"This one's a meaty one," I quipped to Brian over my shoulder, feigning a butcher's ease with the entrails that presented themselves so readily.

"Yeah, thought we should get at least one good roaster from the day," said Brian.

"Roaster?" I queried. "You mean rooster, right?"

"Nope," he said, nonchalantly. "That one's a hen. That one is Susie."

I froze. *Susie, this bird was Susie?*

My daughters and I had bought Susie as a two-day-old chick the previous Easter and had raised her, first in our living room, then in the playhouse, until she was four months old and finally graduated to the chicken coop. Glossy black, with a speckled brown head, she was a beautiful bird. Evidently, she had been a last-minute addition to the slaughter roster.

I fought back feelings of betrayal and the wave of nausea that suddenly washed over me as I mentally composed a Center memo concerning the protocol for future meat harvesting so that would-be pets might escape beloved Susie's fate.

Gritting my teeth and refusing to be undone by the harsh realities of farm life, I began to pull out Susie's intestines and toss them in the garbage. Then my fingers clamped onto something hard. I pulled it out and discovered it was an egg—a beautiful brown egg. I reached in again and pulled out another egg. This one smaller and paler. Again my hand went in and again out came an egg, still smaller and a bit paler.

A crowd of four A Rocha butchers gathered around me. No one spoke, everyone stared. I felt like a magician pulling miracles out of a hat. In all I pulled out seven eggs that varied in size from a tiny soft white ball to a fully formed, hard, elliptical egg.

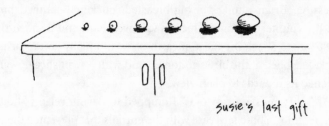

susie's last gift

We were, each one of us, hushed. There before us, spread across the kitchen counter, we beheld the miracle of life itself—and, by extension, the somberness of death. We had killed the goose that laid the golden egg without realizing she was full of golden eggs.

HERITAGE HENS

We no longer eat our layers. And because we let some of them brood and hatch their eggs, we built up quite a flock. Following in the footsteps of the A Rocha chicken wranglers who preceded him, Matt Humphrey, our Center Life Coordinator, chose a heritage breed rather than the factory favorite Rhode Island Reds out of principle for A Rocha's flock. Matt has nothing against Rhode Island Reds, per se, but he does believe that just as biodiversity is important for ecosystems to thrive, genetic diversity is critical for food systems to thrive. This position is supported by a number of agrarian thinkers as well as an important study published in the *Proceedings of the National Academy of Sciences*, which shows that commercial chicken flocks contain about 50 percent of the genetic diversity of their backyard cousins. This lack of genetic diversity is a concern in that it increases the commercial birds' susceptibility to disease. Inbreeding for desirable traits like big breasts or super layers might make economic sense on the industrial scale, but it's tantamount to putting all your eggs in one basket should a new and deadly virus hit the chicken world without the proper genetic umph to resist it. With assistance from Brian the Chicken Guy (not to be confused with Bob the Cow Guy or Brian the Philosopher Cook), Matt developed a humbly impressive flock of over fifty Black Australorpes, a breed developed in the late 1800s in Austria with an eye toward intelligence (which in any chicken is feeble at best), egg laying ability, heartiness, and docility. Back in the early 1900s this breed produced a hen that laid 364 eggs in 365 days, earning it the world record in egg production. Yet because this breed never caught on with industrialized egg farms, their numbers dwindled, qualifying them for "heritage" status—a quaint way of labeling a domestic breed as threatened.

To house our heritage flock Matt and Sean, an uber-able volunteer, built the swankiest chicken coop this side of the Rockies. Based loosely on Joel Saletin's "egg mobile" design, it looks like a little red barn on wheels. The wheels are the key to its ingenuity and practicality, as they enable you to move the coop from one place to another—along with the fact that its floor is made of wire mesh, so that the chickens' waste falls onto the field. This clever little coop provides shelter for the chickens, fertilizer and pest management for the fields, and an aesthetic pleasure for the eye.

DEMONSTRATION EATING

At this point you might be thinking, "Okay, so you've had fun playing farmers and you've figured out how to be really thankful for your food, but, get real, we can't all raise chickens and cows in our backyards! Feedlots are a way of life." True. I'm not naive enough to think that McDonald's is going to go out of business anytime soon. But the question put before us as we started the Center was not, "Should feedlots and fast food restaurants exist?" but rather, "How should we treat *our* cows and what should *we* eat?" We are most certainly concerned with national eating habits, but we are primarily concerned with our own eating habits. We've come to see that if we are brave enough to make the connection between our values and our stomachs, then we must agree with Wendell Berry that eating is an agrarian act that links us directly to plants, animals, and land.

Therefore, we have decided to eat only those animals we have known by name or at least by sight. We realize that this is hardly practical for the common city dweller, but we do it as a sort of best-case scenario for interns and visitors to experience. You've heard of Demonstration Gardens? Well, this is Demonstration Eating! Our hope is that we might gently encourage our guests to be more mindful about where their meat comes from.

HUNTING AND GATHERING

Finally, if meat is on your menu but you can't afford the grass-fed, free-range variety, you might want to consider wild game. By way of a chapter closing, allow me to depart from the farm animal theme to bring you the story of Tashi and his hunter-gatherer exploits.

Tashi is a dear Tibetan man who came to stay with us for two weeks one fall. A conservationist who once kept a snow leopard as a pet (this bit of trivia he offered in response to my girls' question: "Have you ever seen a snow leopard?"), he was delighted in the flora and fauna of British Columbia. Though we didn't have anything as thrilling as snow leopards to show him, Markku and I did take pride in the big and beautiful salmon splashing up the Little Campbell River. Tashi seemed impressed as well. Quite impressed.

A week into Tashi's stay Markku and I left for a two-day conference. We arranged for his activities and his meals, which would all happen within the larger A Rocha community during our absence. There was one meal, however, for which Tashi would have to fend for himself. For that one solitary meal, I left a potato and cheese casserole in the fridge for him to warm up. We returned from the weekend conference to discover the casserole whole and Saran-wrapped in the refrigerator, which we found curious since Tashi seemed to have had a hearty appetite the week previous.

In fact, he did have a very hearty appetite, evidenced by what he ate instead of the meager casserole. We learned later that night that Tashi had waded into the Little Campbell and caught a fifteen-pound Chinook salmon with his bare hands. He killed it by knocking it over the head with a rock and ate it for supper. This was startling news—not because we A Rocha types are opposed to eating salmon, but because this particular salmon was contraband. You see, the stretch of river from which Tashi's salmon was taken lies upstream from a fish hatchery—and in an effort to preserve a vibrant breeding stock, the Department of Fisheries and Oceans Canada has made it illegal to catch any fish that has made it past the hatchery milepost. Given that this salmon was still very much alive when Tashi pulled it from the water, it probably hadn't spawned yet. With only a one in five thousand chance of making it from egg to adult spawner, this Chinook had been taken out of the race within sight of the finish line by an opportunistic Tibetan. Ah, the heartache!

Before Tashi left, the Coho had started their run and were struggling up the river in their own race against time. We stood at the bank, with the water rushing before us, and I told Tashi that these fish were a different species from the one he'd caught. He grew quiet and then looked at me with a twinkle in his eye and asked, "Are they good for eating?"

9

Living Justly, Loving Mercy, Walking Humbly

Do unto others as you would have them do unto you.

JESUS OF NAZARETH

IN MANY COMMUNITIES OF faith it is hip to be poor. Not the missing teeth/body odor kind of poor, but the I'm-skipping-my-latte-today-because-I'm-watching-my-pennies kind of poor. Back when I was a student, we all tried to one-up each other on how "poor" we really were.

"I can't afford the textbook for that class so I have to do all my reading in the library."

Sympathetic nods all around.

"We're so poor we're just going to the water slide park and the aquarium instead of Disneyland."

Tongue clucks all around as we think, "Too bad for you, but I'm *so* poorer!"

This kind of bourgeoisie poverty is not what I want to talk about here. What I want to consider is the living on less than two dollars a day kind of poverty. I used to think, well, those are American dollars. I'm sure two American dollars would go quite a long way in a place like Ethiopia. You could probably pay your rent and get a nice big bowl of lentils for a couple of dollars a day. Then I learned that the dollar everyone was referring to was in the "poor people's" own currency. It didn't pay for rent and dinner; it paid for a bowl of lentils and nothing else.

CONNECTING THE DOTS

If ecology is the study of connections, then the ecologists should be the first to rally against the injustices of environmental degradation and the subsequent human suffering that accompanies it. The reason why many don't, as Peter Harris points out, is that we live in a time of complete disconnection. He writes, "products conceal their origins, academic disciplines operate in expert solitude, social relationships fragment." But the poor do not have the luxury of disconnection from their environment. There are no presto logs to burn when their forests are decimated, no stashes of bottled water when the spring runs dry, no fertile fields around the bend when their crops sizzle during a prolonged drought. Stella Simiyu, a native Kenyan and a Senior Research Scientist in plant conservation at the National Museums of Kenya, writes this about the predicament of the poor.

> If you look at Africa, the rural poor depend directly on the natural resource base. This is where their pharmacy, supermarket, power company and water company are. What would happen to you if these things were removed from your local neighborhood? We must invest in environmental conservation because this is how we enhance the ability of the rural poor to have options and provide for them ways of getting out of the poverty trap.

It is only too easy to live in happy naiveté when it comes to the social and environmental costs associated with our extravagant Western lifestyles. What we need are some clarion voices to draw those connections for us. Re-enter the words of Hosea. Remember?

> Hear the word of the Lord . . . There is no faithfulness,
> no love, no acknowledgement of God in the land. There
> is only cursing, lying and murder, stealing and adul-
> tery . . . Because of this the land mourns . . . the beasts of
> the field and the birds of the air and the fish of the sea are
> dying. (Hos 4:1–3)

If we have eyes to see, then the environmental-suffering-leads-to-human-suffering connection becomes quite apparent, especially in places like Africa and Asia, where the rural poor depend so directly on their local ecosystems for survival. Because the connection is so stark, A Rocha's work in these places always includes a community development component. A Rocha's work in Kenya is a prime example. The team there is working with other conservation organizations and local communities to protect the Arabuke-Sokoke Forest by restoring the link between the well-being of the local ecosystems with the well-being of the people that live in them. Once part of an expansive coastal forest that stretched four thousand kilometers from Somalia to Mozambique, today the Arabuko-Sokoke has shrunk to just at four hundred square kilometers. Still, as the largest and most intact coastal forest remaining in East Africa, it houses one of the richest and most threatened biodiversities in the world. Mida Creek, a tidal inlet, is linked to the Aroabuke-Sokoke by complex natural waterflow systems and has been designated as a UNESCO Biosphere Reserve. Some studies have identified it as one of the most productive mangrove ecosystems on earth.

In an effort to help preserve these ecological gems, A Rocha Kenya has pioneered ASSETS—the Arabuko-Sokoke Schools and Ecotourism Scheme—a holistic conservation intervention that addresses root causes of exploitation and pressures on the Arabuko-Sokoke Forest and Mida Creek, and helps to meet the socio-economic needs of the adjacent communities, where the average per capita income is one dollar per day. ASSETS provides secondary school bursaries, using funds from equitable ecotourism at these sites. When tourists hire A Rocha guides or use the mangrove boardwalks in these locations the money goes directly to a scholarship fund for students from the surrounding villages. The communities, therefore, receive a direct benefit from the conservation of the surrounding ecosystems.

For a span of three years A Rocha Canada received grants from CIDA (Canadian International Development Agency) to send interns to Kenya to assist with this amazing program. Two by two, Canadian university students went and put their conservation and education skills to work directly helping "the poor" by directly helping their environment. It has been our meager offering to those whose poverty makes them so vulnerable to the fluctuations of their surroundings.

MEASURING OUR FOOTPRINT

It seems straightforward to make the connection between conservation and poverty in a place like Kenya, but what about in North America? We can't all go train ecotourism forest guides or put on puppet shows about the dangers of deforestation to Kenya school kids. How can we help? What can we do? In our own lives and work we do some obvious things. We provide a lot of organically grown vegetables for food banks and low-income families. We run day camps and farm days for kids living in poverty. We encourage others to start community gardens. These things are obviously good and worthwhile, but perhaps we need to ask an even better question at the outset—not what can we do, but what can we *stop* doing?

To aid us in the "stopping," a useful tool has been developed which makes the connection between our lifestyle choices here and associated poverty and biodiversity loss elsewhere. This tool is the Ecological Footprint, which measures a person's environmental impact in terms of the productive land needed to support the production of food, materials, and energy as well as the assimilation of waste. This tool takes into consideration everything from carbon output to food consumption and translates one's habits and choices into the tangible evaluative currency of land.

Developed by a team of the researchers at University of British Columbia, the Ecological Footprint of Nations, as it is officially known, gives alarming figures: the average North American requires twenty-four acres of productive land to sustain his/her lifestyle compared to the world average of 5.8 acres. If the global average were to rise to the North American level, we would need approximately five planets to survive! The following is a sampling of Ecological Footprints per average citizen of various countries taken from the Global Footprint Network (www.footprintnetwork.org).

Ecological Footprints around the World

- United States – 24 acres
- Canada – 22 acres
- United Kingdom – 13 acres
- Russian Federation – 11 acres
- Mexico – 6 acres
- World Average – 5.6 acres
- China – 4 acres
- Iraq – 3 acres
- India – 2 acres

Planted

- Bangladesh – 1 acre
- Afghanistan – 0.75 acres

Curious about my own personal environmental impact, I took an ecological footprint quiz found in the back of the book *Radical Simplicity,* by Jim Merkel. My share of the earth: ten acres, under half the American average, which was good news. But I felt like I had fudged some answers (are avocados from Mexico "local" if they come from one's own hemisphere?), and so I went to the guys who developed the Ecological Footprint in the first place—to the Global Footprint Network, which offers a footprint calculator in the form of a fun interactive quiz. For someone who never plays video games, I got a mild buzz watching my little avatar stroll about a fictitious cyber city consuming first one thing than another. I tried to be honest about what I really consumed. Plunk went the trash and recycling in front of my cyber house. Thwack went a bag of groceries as it dropped onto my cyber kitchen counter. My final grade: seventeen global acres—still short of the American and Canadian averages, but horribly above my global "fair share" of approximately six acres. We'd need 3.9 earths instead of five for everyone on the planet to live at my standard. I really had thought I was doing better than this. After all, we recycle everything, drive a wee Honda Civic for our family car, and holiday locally. How could I need seventeen acres and be living so lightly?

Not liking my score and being a skeptic at heart, I decided to get a second and then third opinion. I Googled around and took three similar tests on three different websites. There was a wide variance in results, ranging from four to twelve acres. I found it interesting that the four acres result came from a quiz that was quite simplified and was sponsored by a site that also sold T-shirts, water bottles and camping equipment. (Look how modestly you're living! Don't you feel good? Now, go on and consume some more!) Whatever my score might have been objectively, it was obviously higher than I wanted it to be.

A CHEESEBURGER CASE STUDY

Why do I and my fellow North Americans leave such large footprints? To look at how our everyday life plays out in ecological impact, you don't have to go much further than your own lunch. Consider the cheeseburger. The average American eats around two hundred pounds of beef per year. Nearly all of the cows that became those burgers were born on ranches out west and then transported to large scale CAFOs (Concentrated Animal Feeding Operations) in the Midwest, where they joined literally thousands of their bovine brothers and sisters and were fed primarily corn-based diets until they fattened up to around one thousand pounds. They were then transported to one of the thirteen major slaughter-houses in the nation where they were "processed." Finally the bit of beef that ends up as your cheeseburger was shipped across the country to your local supermarket and found its way to your kitchen table. But the cows are not the only ones on the move. Cattle, designed by the Maker to eat grass, have been redesigned by industrial agriculture to eat corn.

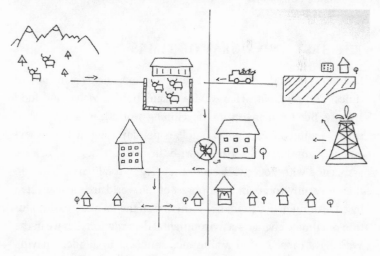

This corn is grown on an industrial scale in places like Iowa using synthetic fertilizer made chiefly of petroleum, harvested with big machinery run on petroleum and then transported from farm to processing plant and then to the CAFOs via rail or highway, using more petroleum. To understand what this means in terms of footprint, consider the following statistics:

- It takes seventy-five gallons of oil to bring a single industrially farmed cow from birth to slaughter.

- Half of all corn and 90 percent of all soybeans are produced for industrial animal farms.

- It takes approximately fourteen pounds of grain to produce one pound of edible beef in the CAFO model.

- Livestock production uses 70 percent of all agricultural land.

- A typical meat eater, dining on primarily factory farmed meat, requires 2.1 acres of farmland to sustain his diet (compared to half an acre for a plant eater).

- Livestock production is responsible for more than one third of the world's methane (twenty-three times as potent a greenhouse gas as CO_2) emissions and two-thirds of its nitrous oxide emissions.

THE BEST AND WORST OF TIMES

In a sense we in the West have been living in a Dickensian "best of times" scenario, with Happy Meals, safe, bottled water, and food aplenty. But for many in the developing world it is "the worst of times." Living on less than two dollars per day, roughly one in seven people in the world struggle with the malnutrition and disease associated with poverty. Because they live in total dependence on their local environment, the poorest of the world are most affected by environmental degradation, whether in the form of toxic pollution or climate change— environmental degradation that we in the West have caused. They are, in fact, innocent bystanders, paying the price for our extravagance.

Where pollution is concerned, the U.S. has outsourced much of its waste. In the chilling documentary *Manufactured Landscapes*,

Edward Burtynsky travels to Fujian and Zhejiang provinces in China in order to photographically document slag heaps, e-waste dumps, and factories, all staggering in their scope. Children and women are seen assembling and de-assembling toxic electronic equipment without the benefit of safety gear as simple as gloves or protective eye-wear. Edward Brown, in his book *Our Father's World,* recounts the implications of corporate bottom lines, which encourage multinationals to locate their factories in countries with little or no environmental regulations—good for consumers up-wind in the more developed countries that receive cheap goods, but disastrous in terms of the toxic pollution for those living near the factories. For example, in 2005, a single toxic spill into the Songhua River in China involved over one hundred tons of benzene, an industrial solvent and carcinogen.

But the effects are not just specific to occasional and localized disasters. There are patterns emerging that are spelling doom for some of the world's most vulnerable. The citizens of the Maldives are watching the oceans rise with increasing apprehension since their country's high point is no more than a mole hill above current sea levels. Their president, who understands the implications of climate change for his country, is reportedly putting a few billion government dollars aside every year in order to relocate his citizens when his country succumbs to the waters—an act of extreme foresight. If his audacious plan works, his compatriots will join the projected 250 million environmental refugees estimated to be on the move by the year 2050.

The plight of the people of Bangladesh, who are among the poorest of all people on earth, is heart wrenching in the extreme. They are caught in a cruel vise that spells a future with not enough good water on one end and too much bad water on the other end. The good water, which flows down the Ganges and Brahmaputra, will begin to dry up as the Himalayan glaciers that feed them melt (which is already happening at alarming rates). The bad water is already encroaching as seawater from the Bay of Bengal floods into the country's agricultural land.

However, it's not just the ruin of crops that is the concern, but the dengue fever, transmitted by a mosquito whose range is expanding due to warmer global temperatures and whose bite often produces the fever that leads to hemorrhaging and death. The *Economist* reported on this phenomena: "Fueled by climate change, dengue fever is on the rise again throughout the developing world, particularly in Latin America. In El Salvador, the number soared to 22,000, a twenty-fold increase of five years earlier. Uruguay recently reported its first case in ninety years."

The list could go on and on. I realize these data sound bites are sensational. I also realize that in many circles, to talk of climate change is to position oneself with a particular political party with particular political agendas. It is not my intent to go to political bat for anyone, nor do I have the pages to outline the climate change argument to a skeptic's satisfaction. If you are curious to learn more, I suggest two particularly helpful and readable books. The first, *Eaarth*, by Bill McKibben, describes both the stunning realities of the new planet we've created and real solutions grounded in hope. (My advice is to start with the "hope" pages in the last third of the book; otherwise you are likely to have nightmares. I did.) The other is *Christianity, Climate Change, and Sustainable Living*, written by Nick Spencer, Virginia Vroblesky, and Robert White. Full of graphs and hard science concerning climate change, this book also lays out the biblical mandate to live sustainably as stewards of God's creation.

And this is what it comes down to in the end: living mindfully as stewards of God's creation. Our brothers and sisters in the developing world are calling us to consider the implications of our lifestyles. They are calling us to consider our fair share of resources. Their plight brings us back to the call of God through Micah—to live justly and love mercy and walk humbly with our Lord. To this end we are to care for the earth and live more simply, because in so doing we care for our less fortunate neighbors.

10

Everything but the Schnitzel

A society in which consumption has to be artificially stimu-
lated in order to keep production going is a society founded on
trash and waste, and such a society is a house built upon sand.

DOROTHY SAYERS

EMBARKING ON A JOURNEY toward simple living is to travel into
uncertain terrain, especially when one is navigating only by the
lay of one's own land. It's easy to feel you've taken the high moral
road when comparing the ecological footprint of your family car
(ours is a fifteen-foot long, fifty-three horse power Honda Civic)
to David Geffen's 453-foot, 50,000-horsepower mega-yacht, but all
self-righteousness is shattered to smithereens when comparing the
selfsame Civic to the family rickshaw in India. And, yes, my home
might be modest in square footage by North American standards,
but compared to an African mud hut, it is palatial.

Simplicity can be a bit of a tightrope walk with pitfalls of self-righteousness on one side and crippling guilt on the other. We can so easily end up like the friend of author Alan Durning, who aptly quipped, "I used to go on shopping trips, now I just go on guilt trips." But despite the hazards, the journey of simplicity is worth taking if we are serious about making the connection between our everyday lives and the everyday lives of everyone and everything else in the world. In many ways, living more simply is the easiest and most practical thing the average North American can do to care for creation and their less fortunate planet-mates. Not many of us can trek to the Outer Hebrides to ring Storm Petrels or set up an orphanage in famine-ravaged Ethiopia, but all of us can shop a little less!

This is a chapter about how we have attempted to walk more lightly on the earth, which is always a two steps forward, one step back sort of tango. Sometimes we're gracefully gliding across the dance floor like environmental Fred Astaires, and the next minute we're thrashing around like we've landed in a mosh pit, but we've tried to keep step to a beat and melody more complex than a strictly North American tune. We've tried to listen for the strains and melodies that call us back to biblical justice and stewardship.

FLYING UPSIDE DOWN

Dallas Willard begins his book *The Divine Conspiracy* with the true story of a test pilot. While practicing a high-speed maneuver in a jet fighter, the pilot turned the controls for what she thought was a steep ascent—and flew straight into the ground, unaware that she had been flying upside down. The story is a stark metaphor for our stuff-addicted lives. When navigating the skies of self-worth and personal satisfaction, most North Americans take their bearings from media and a consumer-driven culture and, in so doing, lose all sense of proportion and reality.

The problem with our society's addiction to stuff is twofold: it's not good for us and it's not good for the world. The issue is essentially one of living humanly and living humanely. The first is spiritual—where we find security and meaning. The second is practical—how we treat the world and those most vulnerable in it.

For me, working and living at A Rocha's Environmental Center has given me a chance to take new bearings and consider my spiritual health. It's a privilege granted to all who come to stay. Interns, many for the first time, realize they've been flying upside down. Time away from usual routines of work and school allow them to slow down, unplug, and recalibrate. This recalibration is the first step in learning to live more simply. It's deep and interior work and is much less about adopting a new fashion (hemp instead of rayon) and much more about adopting a new heart.

For some who've unknowingly been flying upside down, their first few weeks at A Rocha can be a bit unnerving as the G-force of consumerism releases them and they go into a brief free fall before flipping right side up again. For some, this free fall is predicated by an absence of normal routines, including the routine of shopping. Now, we don't have any prohibitions on shopping, it's just that with meals provided and full days of work, whether with vegetables, frogs or school kids, there is neither the need nor the time to nip into the mall on a regular basis. This means that some interns don't visit a store more than once a week or even once a month. Many who come dress as if they are on a perpetual camping trip, so going cold turkey on shopping isn't such a hardship. But for all of us, whether we appear hopelessly out of fashion or are at the height of trendiness, it is so easy to assuage boredom, insecurity, and neurosis with shopping.

LIVING HUMANLY

Shopping as therapy might be a particularly North American phenomenon. I remember sitting in a dorm room in Lithuania with my Lithuanian friends, when three North American students traipsed in after an afternoon at the market. They laid out their purchases—linen clothes, hand-knit socks, wooden spoons—on the beds for us all to admire. After they'd collected their things and left, one of my Lithuania friends turned to me with a bewildered expression on her face and asked, "Is this normal?" At the time I didn't know what she meant. It seemed normal enough to me. She went on to express how strange it was to take such pride in one's purchases and to flaunt them in front of others. She said that in Lithuania, if you really needed something, you went to the market and bought it and that was that.

But I totally "got" these North American students. I grew up in Scottsdale, Arizona in the land of shopping malls and swimming pools. When I was thirteen years old, I owned eighteen Ralph Lauren polo shirts, which I wore two at a time, collars turned up (can you guess the decade?). Each one cost $23.00 and I bought nearly every one with my own money. I have no idea how I made that much money at such a tender age, but do I remember saving for each one and then riding my bike to Scottsdale Fashion Square to plunk down a handful of crumbled bills and sweaty coins in exchange for yet another spanking new polo shirt. I practically fondled my new shirt when I got home, relishing the rush from my brief shopping spree. I had a problem. But I came by my problem honestly—I was an American, raised in the American industrial economy, which depends on a never-ending cycle of production and consumption.

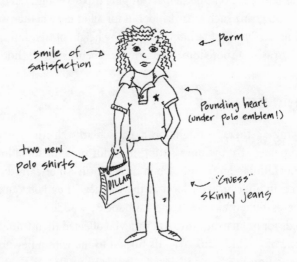

Me - circa 1980

smile of → satisfaction

← perm

← Pounding heart (under polo emblem!)

two new polo shirts →

← "GUESS" skinny jeans

"The industrial economy is the economy of the one night stand," writes Wendell Berry. "I had a good time, says the industrial lover, but don't ask me my last name." The one night stand leaves the consumer with a buzz, but no lasting satisfaction. In this sense, says Berry, the industrial economy's "most marketed commodity is satisfaction, and this commodity, which is repeatedly promised, bought, and paid for, is never delivered." And so the cycle goes, as we trot off to the store for more new stuff to satisfy a craving that the old stuff was supposed to satiate.

Richard Foster puts another spin on this satisfaction theme, contending that our thirst for "more" stems from lacking a divine center. He writes, "We really must understand that the lust for affluence in contemporary society is psychotic. It is psychotic because it has completely lost touch with reality. We crave things we neither need nor enjoy." I would add, enjoy in *the long run*. We certainly enjoy the initial rush, the initial buzz of satisfaction. The problem, as Berry points out, is that the satisfaction is fleeting because we have been brainwashed to crave. Hence, eighteen polo shirts when two would have sufficed.

Time to push pause and insert a little disclaimer: I desire things I both need and enjoy or just plain enjoy but don't need. I'm not advocating Egyptian asceticism where we all rush out to trade in our Lulu Lemon clothes and craftsman style houses for loincloths and pillars. The ballast to extreme asceticism is the doctrine of creation. The stuff of the material world is not innately bad! As outlined earlier, through the incarnation God became stuff. He also made stuff. He was not a disembodied spirit, but a man of flesh and bone accused of gluttony and drinking. He was a carpenter who worked with wood, for *goodness* sake. There is an affirmation of the material world throughout scripture and in Jesus's own life and work. But there are also significant warnings about the love of money and the potential of the heart's ensnarement in the pursuit of those things that "moth and rust destroy." And, of course, there's the admonition to care for the poor and to care for creation. Therefore, it's a "both/and" tension we are called to live in—celebrate the "stuff" of creation, but don't make it your treasure, for there your heart will be also.

CHUCKING THE LEDGER

What I'm striving for in my own daily life is true simplicity, characterized not by deprivation, but by honest, joyful living. Out of this place of joy and material simplicity one is able to question both consumer trends and one's own desires. We are freed to look more honestly at the roots of our dissatisfaction and cravings—freed to consider what will truly satiate the niggling hunger inside. When we can do this we are able to resist the humiliation of the consumer one night stand because satisfaction comes from a deeper source.

If we live in this sort of freedom, we are also released from making simplicity a goal in of itself. Let's face it, living lightly as an all consuming goal is so tempting because the mileposts can be so clear. Reduce garbage from three bags per week to one. Check. Buy birthday gifts at fairtrade market instead of mall. Check. Borrow dress for friend's wedding instead of buying a new one. Check. The danger, of course, is that with each category checked off, the sense of moral righteousness inflates with it, until we've lost the wonder of gratitude and the joy of simple living and are instead focused on our own accomplishments. But pride always cometh before the fall! Allow me to illustrate.

Being leaders of a national Christian conservation organization, Markku and I occasionally get to play host to leaders of other national Christian conservation organizations. It's a pretty small fraternity and while there are no secret handshakes to signify one's membership in this elite club, there are plenty of other signifiers. Like, for instance, turning one's living room into a laundromat.

"Ah, I see you're using a laundry line," Mr. Environmental CEO observes as I show him and his wife into our home.

"Why, yes," I say, practically pawing the ground with my toe.

"In your living room no less!" remarks the wife, with obvious approval.

"The environment's more important than aesthetics," I chirp.

"Indeed," everyone harmonizes in sympathetic agreement.

We weave through our 800-square-foot dwelling to the kitchen, and I can tell they are taking mental stock of our possessions and lack thereof. Feeling very chuffed about our obviously moderate ecological footprint, I brew up some fair-trade, organic loose-leaf tea, and we start in on the favorite topic of all Environmental CEOs everywhere—the evils of a consumer society. We bash all the billionaires we can think of for their private jets, mega mansions, and fleets of Hummers. What hedonists!

Conversely, what enlightened souls this guy and his wife are! So perceptive when it comes to society's ills. So bang on. They are truly so very likeable. I start to wonder if we can set up some sort of arranged marriage between our children so that we can spend all our future Christmases together.

In the middle of my reverie, Mr. Environmental CEO shifts the conversation. To dishwashers. Not the billionaires' uber-delux dishwashers, but the average citizen's plain old dishwashers. *Such energy hogs*, he says. And, *whatever happened to the good ole days of hand washing dishes*? And, *how about redirecting the money people spend on electricity to feeding the poor*? The litany goes on and on, and I begin to feel more and more like a kid caught with her hand in the proverbial cookie jar; for, all the while this guy is musing, I am trying to magically inflate myself like a puffer fish so as to conceal what I am standing right in front of—our brand new Bosch ultra-quiet dishwasher, which I love to pieces.

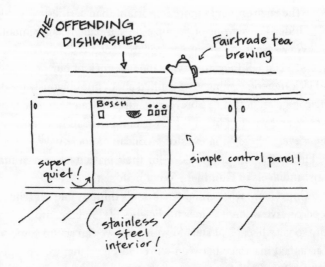

There's always a rub. Forgo the Hummer, but buy the dishwasher. Forgo the dishwasher, but fly fifteen hundred miles to visit your parents every Christmas. And so on. If outward simplicity is the be-all, end-all goal, then the ledger of gains and losses will never balance to anyone's satisfaction.

A word to the wise: throw out the ledger and foster inward simplicity, out of which will flow the freedom to both embrace the wonderful physicality of the world and its gifts, but also the power to resist consumerism's mirage of satisfaction promised through the purchase of material goods.

DOING IT RIGHT

Someone in our community who figured out how to live lightly without all the one-upmanship or ledger tallying was Jessica Nye Brouwer. With her itty bitty A Rocha salary she bought a humble little house on a nearby First Nations Reservation. The 700-square-foot panabode boasted a peek-a-boo ocean view and cost about the same as our Honda Civic. Its affordability lay in the fact that it was situated on a section of the Reservation that provided very tenuous land leases. That, and it had no indoor plumbing. In truth, Jessica's home was plumbed, but the pipes were not connected to anything helpful like a sewer system or water lines. Thus, her drinking and bathing water was trucked in and stored in a big outside tank, and a composting toilet served as her commode. Now, I've heard that some composting toilets are quite decent, but words are inadequate to describe this one. Not surprisingly, Jessica was immoderately proud of this monstrosity. And it was a monstrosity—it had a little mechanical arm in the bowl, which stirred the contents every time you closed the lid, sort of an ultra-revolting KitchenAid mixer. And, of course, being a novelty, no one in Western North America knew how to fix the thing when it broke—which it did, propelling Jessica into the delicate and disgusting art of composting toilet maintenance.

Jessica took the same frugal approach to all her stuff. She had taken a practically monastic vow toward possessions, deciding to buy nothing retail besides food and other absolute necessities for living. Therefore, all her clothes were hand-me-downs or came from thrift stores, and her home was furnished in the style of garage-sale retro. Even items one would think would be impossible to acquire second-hand would find their way into her possession. For example, one day at lunch an intern commented on her groovy "Elvis Costello" glasses.

"Found them," she said, an obvious twinkle of delight in her eyes.

"Found them? Really?"

"Yeah, I lost my glasses and needed new ones," she explained in her gentle voice.

She paused and everyone around the table leaned in for the punchline.

"And I found these," she stated simply.

"Huh? Where? How?" came the chorus of the curious.

"On the beach," she explained. "I found them half buried in sand, took them home, popped out the old lenses, delivered them to the optometrist, and had her put in lenses with my new prescription."

Clever!

The ballast to Jessica's frugality was her love of gift giving. In this way she knew how to live humanly from a place of inner simplicity. Because Jessica was free from the compulsion of shopping, she delighted in the challenge and even joy of living lightly; but, because simplicity itself was not her ultimate goal, she also delighted in purchasing thoughtful gifts for those she loved. True, the gifts were almost always "environmentally friendly" (handmade aprons purchased at the farmer's market or fairtrade chocolate or CDs by local artists), but they were gifts nevertheless—material things that were not absolutely necessary for the recipient's survival, but physical and sentimental tokens that communicated her care and appreciation.

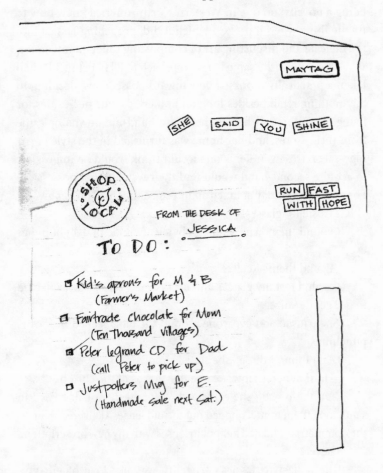

LIVING HUMANELY

I find grocery shopping such a demoralizing experience that I like to do it alone. After spending the last dregs of my emotional energy navigating the cornucopia of pre-packaged, processed food items that the typical grocery store offers up, I simply don't have the stamina to endure the cashier candy gauntlet with kids in tow. But sometimes it can't be avoided and a child must come along. A while back I took my daughter Bryn. We went to one of those really big grocery stores with really big bags of pasta and towering pyramids of caramel-covered everythings. Bryn was enthralled. I guess because she had been left at home during almost all previous grocery expeditions, she was unprepared to encounter the sheer volume of food choices.

On the way home she piped up from the back seat, "Wow, that store had so much stuff. I can't believe how much stuff they had. So much stuff! They had everything!"

She paused and then added thoughtfully, "Except maybe schnitzel. I didn't see any schnitzel."

Then after another pause, "What is schnitzel anyway?"

Thus we come to the second prong of the argument for living simply—living humanely. Living humanely has to do with the rest of the world, a world that is suffering because we are consuming too much stuff—consuming, in fact, everything but the schnitzel! There is no denying our Western lifestyles are extravagant. Our houses are, on average, twice the size they were fifty years ago. Our car journeys take the typical North American on five transatlantic trips each year, and our overall energy use is five times what our grandparents used. Our closets and cupboards overflow with stuff, much of it produced by people living in poverty.

And so we arrive back at the Ecological Footprint.

The hard reality is that we are currently overshooting the earth's bio-capacity by 20 percent. We passed the magic tipping point in 1978. No alarm bells sounded, but in that year, the consumption by the human population outstripped the carrying capacity of earth. We are now living on environmental credit with no plan for repayment.

America's share of worldwide consumption is a 24 percent—a number particularly staggering when one considers that the American population comprises only 5 percent of the global community. We are the world's greatest consumers. A quick snapshot of statistics tells the tale of a society awash in trash and unsustainable consumption.

Americans "consume":

106,000 aluminum cans every thirty seconds

15 million sheets of office paper every five minutes

426,000 cell phones every day

3.6 million SUVs per year.

The raw materials for each sheet of paper, microchip, and radial tire must be harvested from forests, soils and rocks. Enormous quantities of water and energy are expended in both their production and transportation. The result, as we saw in the previous chapter, is degraded ecosystems, desertification, shrinking habitats and a Developing World at the service of the Developed World. Photographer Chris Jordan, from whom these statistics come and who produced a fascinating photographic collection titled *Intolerable Beauty* that documents America's waste, has this to say about North America's consumer habits: "Collectively we are committing a vast and unsustainable act of taking, but we each are anonymous and no one is in charge or accountable for the consequences. I fear that in this process we are doing irreparable harm to our planet and to our individual spirits."

Time to screw up our courage and acknowledge that when we tug on the thread of our extravagant consumption the web quivers all over the planet in the form of species extinction, climate change, and social injustice.

A WAY FORWARD

We North Americans love prescribing solutions. Just give us a recipe for Ten Easy Steps to This or That and we feel secure. The Living Lighter Ten-Step Program usually includes things like changing light bulbs, taking the bus, turning off lights, lowering the thermostat. All good and important actions, but such pre-scriptions miss the point that our root problem is our addiction to consumption. To just tweak one or two small actions does little to relieve the overall planetary stress we've created. Our earth simply can't accommodate all the trash, nor provide all the resources, nor absorb all the carbon required by our stuff-addicted lives. So rather than ending with a To Do list, I'd like to leave you with three practices that encourage joyful, simple living.

1. Practice Gratitude

When we were just starting out with A Rocha and before we had moved to the Environmental Center, we hosted Japanese homestay students as a way of both augmenting our income and also trying our hand at community living. Yuko came to stay with us for six months. She was gentle and kind and full of reflections about all the new things she was learning during her time in Vancouver. One night, after we'd said grace before dinner, she looked at us thoughtfully and remarked, "I'm so glad you say a prayer before dinner." She went on to explain how she had always felt a need to say thanks to someone—for food, for friends, for all that she had. Her gratitude was like a balloon inside her, welling up, but with nowhere to go, because she didn't know to whom or what she should address her thanks. Then she said, "Now I know whom to thank."

"Gratitude is the heart of faith," writes Mary Jo Leddy. In this vein, she relates a lovely prayer of gratitude the Jewish people pray every Passover as they celebrate the deliverance of the Hebrew people from Egypt. The prayer centers around the Hebrew word *Dayenu*, which in English means, *It would have been enough.*

- If you had only led us to the edge of the Red Sea but not taken us through the waters, *it would have been enough.*

- If you had only taken us through the Red Sea but not led us through the desert, *it would have been enough.*

- If you had only led us through the desert but not taken us to Sinai, *it would have been enough.*

Leddy suggests using this template as a helpful spiritual exercise in reflecting on one's own life. For example: If I had only been born but not had a twin sister, *it would have been enough.* If I had only had a twin sister but hadn't visited Orcas Island, *it would have been enough.* If I had only seen the sun set off Otter's Point on Orcas Island, but hadn't experienced a snowfall in the Rockies, *it would have been enough.*

When we are satisfied with our lives as *being enough,* we are able to resist the whispers of consumerism that tell us we don't have enough or we *are* not enough. When our sense of satisfaction is rooted in an amazement at the givenness of every gift—from friends to home to our very own lives—then we are grounded in the firm grace of abundance.

Gratitude's starting point is wonder. I love what the Jewish theologian Abraham Heschel says about true spiritual living: "Our goal should be to live life in radical amazement." He encouraged his students to take nothing for granted. "Everything is phenomenal; everything is incredible; never treat life casually. To be spiritual is to be amazed." The amazement comes as we realize everything we have and every gift we experience is pure grace. To be born would have been enough, but then I'm given a loving family. Wow! To be raised in a loving family would have been enough, but then I am surrounded by caring mentors. Amazing! We are invited not only to consider the big gifts, but the little gifts as well—the light slanting through the fir trees on a fall afternoon or the caress of a small child's hand on our arm. It's all grace. It's all amazing. It all warrants our gratitude.

2. Practice Generosity

Once upon a time Markku and I owned a big house with an ocean view. It was the antithesis of Jessica's humble panabode. It had hardwood floors, two fireplaces, more bedrooms and bathrooms than necessary and was comprised of three very livable "suites." We took the biggest mortgage we could afford and rented all the suites, which more than covered the bills. It was, in fact, a cash cow. It never went un-rented, was incredibly easy to maintain, and generated a modest income above the cost of the mortgage.

I loved that house. Not to live in myself, mind you—it was way too grown-up and refined for that. If I lived *there* someone might think we were rich! No, what I loved about that house was the financial security it represented. Drawing an A Rocha salary that hovered right around the Canadian poverty line, I found solace as I mentally calculated how much our house would be worth in five, ten, or twenty years. In my imaginings, the house transformed itself into neat and sparkling stacks of gold coins and I, like a miserly Silas Marner, brooded over that treasure, rubbing my knuckly hands together while cackling, "Mine, all mine!"

And then one morning, as we were eating our oatmeal, Markku said, "I've been thinking."

I knew I was in for something big, because *I've been thinking* is the introductory phrase Markku most often uses whenever proposing one of his more outlandish ideas. For example: *I've been thinking, we should get married*; or, *I've been thinking, we should quit our jobs and work for A Rocha;* or, this time, "I've been thinking, we should sell our house and invest in the A Rocha bonds."

The A Rocha Board had hatched a plan to pay back the loan to the Leitzes through bond offerings secured against the Center property. Essentially, through bonds, A Rocha would receive a privately financed second mortgage at 5 percent interest. A handful of people thought this was a fine idea and had plunked down money, but we still needed a sizable chunk of cash to pay out the Leitzes.

His suggestion was like a punch in my gut. It was if he had marched into my little fantasy and kicked my tidy stacks of gold coins across the room.

So I did what I always do when presented with an outlandish idea from Markku: I said I'd think about it. And think about it I did, mostly while taking long walks around the neighborhood. As I walked, I prayed. And as I prayed, I clenched and unclenched my hands and raised them heavenward. I'm sure if anyone saw me, they must have thought I was into some funky sort of Tai Chi, but the gesture served as a physical way to release what I knew had taken possession of my heart.

And so I agreed to put our ocean-view house on the market. It took forever to sell, and as the housing market bubble started to deflate and our asking price continued to decrease, I second-guessed my moment of spiritual magnanimity that had allowed me to say yes to Markku's house-selling proposal. But in the end, I stuck to my intuition that this was the best thing, not only for A Rocha, but also for me personally, for with this choice I would grow in freedom and inner simplicity.

Inward simplicity, I suggest, is hallmarked by a joyful detachment from possessions. It has nothing to do with the abundance or lack of possessions. It has everything to do with trust. With the sale of our home, I stopped fantasizing about my future fortune and started trusting that all would be well come retirement day.

When it comes to outward simplicity, I still have a long way to go to pair down my seventeen global acres (or was it four?) to something more globally sustainable. I realize that the only way I'm going to travel further in this journey is by making choices, some of them hard. Many of those choices will require sharing. Of course, not all my decisions to share need to be as huge as selling our house. Currently we share a phone line with our upstairs housemates. We share a lawn mower with five other families. We share meals, clothes, and time with friends and neighbors. All this sharing is a practical way for us to break free from the "culture of scarcity" so prevalent in North America, where, somehow, despite our incredible abundance, we have absorbed the idea that we need more, that there's not enough, that it's dangerous to be generous. Sharing combats this neurosis by putting us in a place of trust that enables us to release our grasp on possessions. Sharing allows us to unclench our fists and enjoy the abundance found in generosity.

3. Practice Keeping the Sabbath

My family keeps the Sabbath. Not religiously—as in, we don't always do religious things. But we are pretty religious about "keeping" it. Usually we go to church. Usually we eat simply—eggs and toast is normal fare for Sunday dinners. Usually we say "no" to invitations and engagements unless they involve family. If it's winter we might go cross-country skiing; if it's rainy we might read a book aloud as a family; if it's sunny we might take a walk at the beach. Our only hard and fast rule is no shopping. The point is, we say "no" to certain things. We step out of our normal rhythms of work and commerce and step into a new way of being.

The main challenge of Sabbath keeping is precisely this slowing down, this stripping of the normal routines that keep us humming (and mask the dissonance in our lives). My personal challenge is saying "no" to the computer. By about four in the afternoon on any given Sunday I start to feel fidgety and I begin to feel the pull of technology. My computer begins to send out subliminal messages from its corner cupboard, wooing me to check my e-mail or tinker on an article due the following week. Some Sundays I practically have to sit on my hands to keep from turning it on. But when I resist, I am rewarded with fresh eyes and a sense of proportion about myself and the world.

Essentially, the Sabbath is about time. It's about trusting in a rhythm of time that depends not on clocks attuned to commerce, but on a larger clock attuned to the rhythms of nature and of God. Sabbath is rooted first in the Jewish notion of day, which in their calculation begins at sundown. Thus, we go to sleep as the day is just getting rolling. We wake when the day's half over. In a society where productivity is the measure of worth, it would seem counter intuitive to begin one's day by lying down and shutting one's eyes.

The beginning of day is for writing lists, making plans, springing from the starting blocks, not for putting on one's pajamas. But in the Jewish creation narrative, the day begins not with the rising of the sun, but with its setting—there was evening, there was morning, the first day. The day begins with rest and is followed by work, a work already begun by God, and into which humans join.

...day is begun, gone the sun...

The Sabbath is also rooted in the Jewish understanding that this particular day is a different sort of day, not only in its parameters, but in its essence. The Jewish creation narrative, Abraham Heschel says, states that the first thing in all of creation that is declared holy is the Sabbath—not a people or a place, but a day. Everything else in creation is declared good, but this day, the seventh day, is declared holy. The Sabbath, then, becomes a "palace in time," into which we are invited. The invitation, writes Heschel, is to come away from the "tyranny of things of space" to "share what is eternal in time, to turn from the results of creation to the mystery of creation." The Jewish image of the Sabbath is of a window into the kingdom of God. It is a day to tap into our instincts for eternity, for something bigger than the concrete and commercial stuff of our everyday lives.

As we train our gaze to a horizon beyond the consumer habits of our society, the Sabbath becomes a day of refashioning. The recalibration that occurs spills into the rest of the week as we shift away from a consumer-driven way of living toward a relational way of living. Indeed, as I've come to recognize the holiness of this one day and as I've gazed through this weekly window into the eternal by simply stopping and resting, I've begun to realize that God has left windows open throughout the week through which a Sabbath draft flows. Moments are found to realign, to practice that art of saying no, to resist the temptations of competition and consumerism.

As a parting offering in these Sabbath musings I offer a short poem written while reflecting on a metaphor common in Jewish lore, where the Sabbath is compared to a queen. Thus, just as one would roll out the red carpet for a royalty, so one honors this day as the queen of days.

The Sabbath Queen

The days are drones and swirl
about my head,
darting, drumming in my ears.
Beneath them I squat,
swollen with the sting of their concerns
of commerce and competition.

I heave myself
from place to place,
but find nowhere to rest;
all is bustle and business,
when what I need is binding up
of wounds and worries.

But then I come to her—
regal in her unconcern
for the frenzied course I've taken.
She is midwife to my frustration,
birthing the stillborn cares,
which she sets aside, swaddled in a solitary
place I do not know.

In their stead she offers

Planted

nothing but a place to sit and rest.
And in that rest I am refashioned—
unswollen; the poison of the days transfused
with a nectar sweet and satisfying,
so that when I rise to bid her well,
I am well.

11

Manna for Each Day

God's gifts put man's best dreams to shame.

Elizabeth Barrett Browning

The problem with loans is that they must be repaid. The initial interest-free loan from the Leitzes for A Rocha's first environmental center required monthly payments of $5,000. The amount seems almost laughably small now, when our annual budget has grown by about 1,000 percent to what it was then. But at the time, $5,000 was a significant amount of money. We made the first three payments, no sweat. But then Christmas rolled around and the world seemed distracted by their holiday to-do lists, which obviously did not include a line for "send donation to the upstart charity, A Rocha." December 31 arrived around, and we were still $5,000 short of the payment that was due the next day. It was late afternoon, and Markku and I were running errands and fretting.

So soon, we thought.

We'd just have to call the Leitzes and break it to them. "Thanks for your good faith in us, but we don't have the money. So sorry, maybe next month."

We knew three months in, this scenario would be a disappointment to everyone. As we ran through various confessional scenarios, Markku noticed a stack of mail tucked in between the dashboard and the windshield. It was mail I had collected the day before and, not being an administrative type, had filed under "D" for dashboard. Markku began opening letters, and out of the first envelope fell a check. A check for $5,000 from a foundation halfway across the country—a foundation we had never approached, not for so much as a dime. Ask any fundraiser, foundations do not make a practice of sending out unsolicited checks. We were humbled, stunned, and very grateful.

Still, even with this miraculous provision, every month that first year was a test of faith. Month quickly followed month like hurdles barely crossed until we were staring our one-year finish line square in the face. With that anniversary came the deadline to repay our loan from Grandview Calvary Baptist: one hundred thousand dollars—in one installment. Markku made phone calls, lots of people prayed and I kept my fingers crossed while my faith waxed and waned. There was really nothing I could do except go on with life that on one particular afternoon entailed pushing our girls on the swings. As I pushed I saw Markku emerge from the A Rocha office across the driveway. He walked slowly and deliberately across the lawn. I remember he had a funny look on his face, a look that implied weighty news. As he got closer I noticed that he also had tears in his eyes. My heart started to beat faster. I abandoned the swing set and my dangling daughters and met him halfway across the yard.

"I just got off the phone with Peter Harris," he said.

I instantly thought something had happened to Miranda—a car accident, I was sure.

"He said he found us a donor who'll give us the $100,000."

I gaped. And I nearly fell over from relief, mostly because Miranda was not dead, but also because of the miracle of provision.

There have been times that this drama of fundraising has felt like an Old Testament soap opera. The tribe, with gnawing bellies, has been grumbling, and manna has dropped seemingly out of the sky so that the only explanation must be that it has come from the hand of God. But like the manna of old, it hasn't "kept." It's been good just for the day it was needed, and the weeks and even months that followed these days of bounty were more often days of drought.

Those drought days taught us to pray. During their tenures in the office, Jessica and Tiina paused in their work every day at three in the afternoon to do just this. Jessica's prayers were simple: "God, send us a million dollars." That's what we needed, so that's what she prayed. But the donations stayed small, even if they were steady. And I went back to wrestling with the demons of the importance of our work. There were just so many worthy causes and so many people suffering around the world that I felt guilty for adding another cause to anyone's charitable giving plate, especially for a cause that, at the time, seemed frivolous because it didn't directly save the starving. What finally came to me during one particular time of wrestling prayer was the image of Mary pouring perfume on the feet of Jesus. In reflecting on this reckless act of adoration and Jesus' refusal to condemn Mary for wasting on him what could have been spent on the poor, I understood once again that God doesn't do triage. I also perceived Jesus' delight in a small thing done with great love, to borrow Mother Teresa's phrase. A Rocha's Environmental Center was a small extravagant thing, done with great love. God would use it, in fact, to care for the poor through the sharing of food and through the transformed lives of those who have chosen to live more simply.

THE MANITOBA STORY

While we were still in those early days of fundraising and some of the more faith-filled were praying their million-dollar prayers, we got an email from Henry Martens in Manitoba. He said he would be out in Vancouver for a conference that A Rocha was hosting in partnership with Regent College, and he wanted to chat.

He didn't have a million dollars in his back pocket, but he did have a remarkable story. During the span of thirty years he had amassed over six hundred acres of environmentally sensitive land in the Pembina Valley of Manitoba with the dream of starting a Christian nature center that would promote dependence and connection to the land and to the Creator. We later learned from locals that Henry had a bit of a Noah reputation. While others of his set might have been buying bigger houses or taking extravagant holidays or saving for retirement, Henry was buying land. Land on the bluffs of the Pembina Valley, rich in Burl Oak, porcupine, and mule deer. Land that led down to the Pembina River. He bought this land, parcel by parcel, from those farmers willing to sell (and there were plenty that weren't, even though the land was impossible to farm given its steep slope). Neighbors would scratch their heads and wonder what this crazy coot was up to amassing all this un-farmable land. Thirty years later Henry and his wife Elma had so much land that they were able to sell, at cost, five hundred acres to the Manitoba government for a provincial park. Another tract of land was donated to a Christian summer camp, which left approximately one hundred acres for their dream of a nature center.

Enter A Rocha and another key character in the story: Paul Goossen. A wildlife biologist raised in the Pembina Valley, but living in Edmonton, Paul was passionate about creation and studying birds of prey in particular. Because the Pembina Valley falls in one of North America's premier raptor migration corridors, he was curious what sort of studies could be done there. Eager to make connections he contacted Henry, whom he knew as the guy with the crazy idea for a Christian nature center. He called and asked if he could stop in for a visit and was invited for coffee.

On the day of his visit he was escorted in and left to settle into an armchair while Henry and Elma gathered drinks in the kitchen. As he waited, he fished in his satchel for a brochure. As Henry left the kitchen en route back to Paul, he fished in his desk drawer for a brochure. Simultaneously they both handed each other the very same brochure—for the upcoming A Rocha/Regent College Conference on creation care in Vancouver—with the same words, "There's something I wanted to show you." Stunned, they took it as confirmation that they should travel to Vancouver together.

Markku met them both at the conference and heard their story over dinner. They proposed that A Rocha purchase Henry's remaining land and set up a center similar to the one we were creating on the B.C. coast. Of course, it was madness to think A Rocha Canada was ready for another project when we were weren't even out of the crawling stage with the first center. We consulted Peter Harris. His advice—"Don't run before you can walk"—was extremely sage, but as we learned more of Henry's story, it was hard not to think that this big miraculous ark had just put into port. However, to extend the metaphor, it'd be sailing again soon, and we'd be crazy not to jump aboard. And so we stood at the dock and considered the leap. More discussions were held, a formal proposal was submitted, and with the Board's blessing and bidding—and with a significant leap of faith—A Rocha Prairie Canada was born.

Of course, a property does not a project make. Because Henry and Elma were already at retirement age, they were in need of a band of supporters and volunteers who would help make their dreams a reality. They also knew that they would eventually need an individual or couple to whom they could pass on the running of this new center. Therein lay another need for provision: people. Enter Larry and Myra Danielson, a couple with a penchant for tooling around the Pembina Valley backroads in the dead of winter. On one such minus-thirty-degrees outing their car skidded off the road and landed in a snowdrift. Noticing that they were not far from the Provincial park, Larry huffed through the snow in search of aid. Myra waited patiently in the car for rescue as her wheelchair sat idly in the trunk. That rescue came in the form of Henry and his Kubota tractor. In no time Henry had pulled the car and its grateful owners from the drift. And because in rural Manitoba you invite strangers into your home like the long lost relatives they might be, Henry invited the Danielsons in for tea.

As Larry and Myra were treated to warm drinks and goodies by Elma and Henry, they learned about A Rocha and the work to transform the Marten's former home into the Pembina Valley Field Station. They got excited about this prospect and in time became two of A Rocha Prairie Canada's most faithful volunteers. And because they are both incredibly diligent and well-connected, they have drawn in a wonderful array of supporters and volunteers, including Susan and Nick Pharaoh, who took the reins of the field station's leadership for a critical three-year period. This sort of recruiting and staffing is hardly a strategic plan that could have been scripted, or approved by a Board of Directors, for that matter. The unfolding of A Rocha in the Prairies has been more like an Old Testament narrative, as provision has seemingly sprouted from rock and been pulled from snowdrifts.

BACK TO B.C.

We learned from our experience with the project in Manitoba that big things start inconspicuously—more often than not, in innocence and seeming chance. Therefore we shouldn't have been surprised when years later the same principle played out back in B.C.

From our vantage, that small inconspicuous moment came one summer morning as I wandered about the Center with a very young Maya and Bryn. Because they were so young, they still had the gift of living totally in the present, wandering from dandelion to tree frog to ant with the fascination of trained ecologists. And I wandered after them, drifting in the wake of their explorations. Our meanderings were interrupted by a car that pulled into the Center parking area. A tall woman with the air of retired ballerina emerged, followed by two preteen girls. The woman introduced herself as Brenda Neufeld and her daughters as Emily and Elizabeth. She said she'd heard about A Rocha from someone at her church and wondered if she might have a look around.

I happily offered to give them a tour and we set off around the gardens, through the forest grove and down to the ponds. As we looped around the bigger of the two ponds, Maya snatched a tree frog from the long grass. Brenda seemed delighted. "Oh, my girls do that!" she exclaimed. As we came to the far corner of the property I pointed down to the Little Campbell River and she remarked, "Oh, so the river doesn't actually flow through your property?" I remember feeling apologetic about this geographical oversight on the part of A Rocha and said something about it being on the neighbors' land, but having permission to do environmental studies there. She seemed especially curious about the river.

We ended the tour back in the parking area. Her daughters played tag with mine. There was a tangible spark of kinship between us all. As she was departing Brenda mentioned that she had lambs and wanted to know if I'd like to bring the girls over to see them. We exchanged phone numbers but didn't set a date.

Being relatively new to the area and having nary a friend, I immediately took Brenda up on her invitation to hang out with her sheep. I'm not usually so bold as to call a person I've just met and invite myself over, but the allure of lambs was too great and I phoned. Brenda seemed thrilled to hear from me, but she didn't invite us to see the lambs; instead she invited us to meet her at her mother's house at Brooksdale, an estate about three miles up-river from the Center. So the following week the girls and I headed to the mysterious "Brooksdale" for a tea party.

Arriving at Brooksdale was like stepping out of suburbia and into a Jane Austen novel. Heritage Tudor-style buildings, including a coach house, stables, cottages, and a manor house, dotted the palatial grounds. Magnificent Douglas fir trees buffered the residences from the road, and an iconic yellow barn rose from the fields. In a word, the place was stunning. We parked and approached the manor house and saw that it overlooked a beautiful stretch of the Little Campbell River.

Brooksdale

Brenda, her mother, and her mother's German care-giver, Ute, warmly welcomed us. Maya and Bryn drank from miniature antique tea cups as we nibbled cookies. The whole atmosphere was one of utter civility and old world hospitality. I half-expected Elizabeth Bennet to pop through the swinging butler's door to inquire after the health of our relatives and offer us all crumpets.

I returned home as if from a dream. After describing the wonders of the place and the company to Markku, I remember exclaiming, "Now *that's* an A Rocha Center!" Markku was scandalized. He said something about bigger and better and the American way and about how we already had a center and to be content. I defended myself by saying I didn't actually think A Rocha should *be* at Brooksdale, just that it would, hypothetically speaking, make an amazing environmental center—hypothetically speaking. Never in my wildest dreams could I have imagined A Rocha and Brooksdale in the same sentence, let alone the same address.

Over the course of time, Markku and our A Rocha colleagues also formed a relationship with the Neufelds. In time we were

invited to conduct conservation science studies and habitat restoration projects at Brooksdale. Our intern Martin set up his small
mammal traps and camped out on the property as he hunted for
the ever-elusive Pacific Water Shrew. Glen Carlson and troops of
volunteers planted hundreds of native plants to enhance wildlife
habitat. And still others dug out a rearing channel along the Little
Campbell for Coho salmon fry.

As all this was occurring we began to learn more about the
Brooksdale property and its fascinating history. Originally built
as an upscale riding estate for a Vancouver lumber baron named
Brooks, the property had more recently served as a care facility for
people suffering from mental illness and mental disabilities. Without a shred of experience in the field, the Neufeld family took over
the work in the early 1970s and ran it as a family business until the
late 1990s. When they first arrived, Brenda described the place as
something out of *One Flew Over the Cuckoo's Nest*, with the clients
heavily medicated and peering fearfully out the windows.

Over the years the Neufelds and their hard-working staff
transformed this institutional facility into a place of care. Drama
troops and musical ensembles were formed. Performances were
held in the big yellow barn. The residents also worked in the gardens, helping with the planting, weeding, and harvesting of the
food that would later fill their stomachs. They tinkered with wood
in the workshop and relaxed by the river in the late afternoons.
And, on occasion, they were treated to "family holidays" to Disneyland or Hawaii. When I heard this latter bit of trivia I was
amazed. Who takes their psychiatric patients to Hawaii!? I quickly
realized that the Neufelds and their colleagues had obviously not
been running a business, but a home. Their devotion to their extended family showed in the little things they did—from ironing
their clients' clothes to baking fresh bread every Friday for them
to enjoy. Through each act of care these men were treated with a
dignity that was often denied them in the outside world.

The more I learned the more I realized that the Neufeld family and their staff were a remarkable bunch. The thoughtfulness
with which they approached their clients was extended even to

the land itself. Arnold Neufeld, who had passed away ten years previously, had a strong sense that the land was to be cared for and preserved because it was given by God.

Over the years the family discussed their collective desire to see their property used for Christian ministry that would honor the care they had exhibited in this special place. Of course, we A Rocha-ites had no notion of any of this. Personally, I was simply enjoying the occasional tea parties with Mrs. Neufeld and the friendship Brenda graciously offered. But bit by bit, I began to suspect that the Neufeld family had some sort of surprise up their sleeve. A series of cryptic remarks over a two-year span, when pieced together, began to bring a remarkable picture into view:

Brenda: "I've always thought you were on the wrong property."

Me: *Confused, but feigning otherwise,* "Right."

Brenda: "It's not an accident that we met."

Me: *Confused, but assuming she was talking about Reformed Theology,* "Right."

Brenda: "Things are coming together."

Me: *Confused, but very curious,* "Right."

The conversations were truly this cryptic, and my responses were truly this monosyllabic. Although I had a growing sense that something sensational was "going down," I didn't dare presume that it had anything to do with the aforementioned shared address for A Rocha and Brooksdale. But indeed, this is exactly what the Neufeld family had up their collective sleeve. They wanted to gift a good portion of Brooksdale, including all the heritage buildings and environmentally sensitive habitat, to A Rocha. Brenda presented this bold proposition to a staggered Markku, who returned home bewildered by the sheer generosity of it all. This was certainly beyond the one-million-dollar provision Jessica had been praying for—prayers that had continued because we still owed a considerable amount of money for the first center. A move to Brooksdale would mean not only the opportunity to steward this amazing property, but the freedom to operate an environmental center debt-free.

In order to help with the transition to Brooksdale from the old Center, Markku and I acted as a vanguard. With the arrival of new Center Directors in the form of David and Shauna Anderson, we were freed up to move off-site and set up shop at Brooksdale. The hope was to get to know Mrs. Neufeld better by living on-site, but sadly a few weeks before our own move, she died suddenly and peacefully in her sleep. I had been looking forward to more time for tea and watching *I Love Lucy* reruns together, but it was not to be. Mrs. Neufeld's passing led to a quicker transition, and plans were made for the remaining Center staff, interns, and animals to follow a year after our arrival whereupon we would be released to live offsite.

This transition has come to pass and the journey continues. It's a journey of faith, both for those of us at A Rocha and also for the Neufeld family as they move forward with their intention of donating a portion of their beloved property into our care. There are municipal bylaws to be navigated and an estate to be settled, but the gifting is going ahead as we all hold it with open and grateful hands.

In a sort of happily-ever-after scenario, the first center continues to be stewarded with the level of concern and care with which the A Rocha team tended it. In fact, it was a small collective of A Rocha and A Rocha-esque folks who purchased that property, including our farmer Paul, cow-loving Rick, and ourselves. Together with a few other families we have formed an intentional community with a very symbiotic relationship to Brooksdale as we continue species studies in the ponds and grow food for A Rocha's CSA in the fields.

PEOPLE PROVISION

While the gifts of finances and property have been astounding, an even more astounding provision has come in the form of the people who have been drawn to this work. There have been those who have joined us at our centers—individuals with incredible talent and vision who could be earning double to four times what they earn working for A Rocha, but who believe in the vision of creation care as a Christian calling. Then there are those further flung like Cindy Verbeek, who works tirelessly in a Northern B.C. lumber town, where wearing the label "environmentalist" is akin to affixing a scarlet O (for "odd") to one's chest. Jen Kornelson and Bethany Petkau have pioneered a wonderful project in inner-city Winnipeg that addresses issues of food security, poverty, and justice amongst the city's marginalized. And Paul Abell, Peter Scholtens, and Luke Wilson are gathering a group of like-minded friends in the Greater Toronto Area who are throwing their backs into a wide range of practical conservation projects. Add to these numbers the countless volunteers, who have joined our community garden network across Canada and who are turning church parking lots and lawns into places of bounty and hospitality, and you have a whole movement of people working to show God's love for all of creation in humble and yet significant ways.

THE MYSTERY OF PROVISION

All these people and projects are signs of growth, but more than that, they are signs of God's provision. This sort of provision is a mystery in the best sense of the word, since God is neither a sugar daddy nor a slot machine. I know this, just as I know that prayer is about way more than just making requests. With all my heart I believe that prayer, at its core, is about union with God. Even so, God has responded to our collective prayers for finances and people in ways that cause me to shake my head and marvel at the obvious connection between our asking and our receiving. Every dollar comes as a gift from those who've generously given out of their convictions to care for the earth and their belief that we will use their money to do just that. This is hugely humbling and deeply encouraging. Every colleague who joins us does so sacrificially, giving up the security of pension plans and competitive salaries to do work they wholeheartedly believe in. This is also hugely humbling and deeply encouraging.

Some days I look around at Brooksdale—at this gobsmackingly amazing property—and at the forty staff, interns, and volunteers gathered for lunch around a common table laden with fresh food grown in A Rocha's gardens, and I want to weep for gratitude and awe that what started in a cupboard under a stairwell has become this big, beautiful thing so beyond my imagining. In response to the magnitude of this grace, all I can do is fling my arms wide, lift my chin to the sky, and say a resounding, "Thank you!"

12

In Closing

ONE AFTERNOON I WALKED into an A Rocha outbuilding and found a hummingbird buzzing at the window. Years before, my grandfather's neighbor, the ornithologist, had told me that hummingbirds will become quite still when trapped inside—so still that you could just pick them up, like a piece of cotton.

Remembering Frank Richardson's words, I walked directly up to the window, reached out my hand and closed it gently around the bird. I carried it outside, holding it cupped like a secret wisp of pure energy. Peeking at it through the gap between my index finger and thumb, I saw its breast thrumming with the excitement of its capture. Amazed by its fragile vitality, I cradled it a moment longer. Then slowly, in a gesture of supplication, I opened my hands and raised them heavenward. The hummingbird lingered a full two seconds, free and blinking in the daylight. And then, like a bolt, it shot from its perch, cleaving the air in an iridescent arc.

That was a good day. I tangibly cared for creation by literally saving a creature, and I felt bolstered in my calling and vocation. Other days I walk by faith that our work in creation care is making a difference. On my best days I fall back on Wendell Berry's advice to "be joyful though you've considered all the facts." On my worst days I write eulogies for the ferns outside my front door and am immobilized by the weight of suffering that the poor and innocent carry.

After finishing Bill McKibben's challenging book, *Eaarth*, I descended into eulogy-writing mode.

In my desperation, I shook Markku by his imaginary lapels and cried, "What are we going to do?!"

Calmly, he responded, "We are going to do what is right. We aren't going to save the world, Leah. We are going to do what is right."

At the time of this particular panic episode, we were reading *The Lord of the Rings* out loud to our daughters. I was wallowing in despair over the severity of the environmental crisis and could hardly focus on the story when Markku read the words spoken by Gandalf to Pippen during the battle for Minas Tirith:

> . . . the rule of no realm is mine, neither of Gondor nor any other, great or small. But all worthy things that are in peril as the world now stands, those are my care. And for my part, I shall not wholly fail of my task, though Gondor should perish, if anything passes through this night that can still grow fair or bear fruit and flower again in days to come. For I also am a steward.

Markku paused and found my eyes. We smiled at each other—resigned, sad, and hopeful. We would do what was right. With the hard work and accompaniment of our dear colleagues at A Rocha, we would continue our efforts to save the Little Campbell River, though it's nearly a trickle in the summer months. We would welcome the stranger to A Rocha's environmental centers, though sometimes they are truly strange and inconvenient. We would grow food, without pesticides or herbicides, and feed the hungry. We would choose to live with less so that others might live with more. We would cradle the wayward hummingbirds in our hands and set them free, amazed and grateful for the privilege of doing so.

We would choose joy, though we had considered all the facts.

Sources

(In order of appearance)

CHAPTER ONE: THE STUDY OF HOME

Brett, Brian.*Trauma Farm*. Vancouver, BC: Greystone, 2009.
Muir, John. *My First Summer in the Sierra*. San Francisco: Sierra Club, 1988.

CHAPTER TWO: BACKING INTO THE FUTURE

Lamott, Anne. *Operating Instructions*. New York: Ballantine, 1993.

CHAPTER THREE: SUBTERRANEAN GRACE IN A WORLD OF WOUNDS

DeWitt, Calvin B. *Earth-wise*. Grand Rapids: CRC Publications, 1994.
Brown Taylor, Barbara. *The Luminous Web: Essays on Science and Religion*. Boston: Cowley, 2000.
Fee, Gordon. *Cosmic Pain of Redemption,* a lecture delivered at the Regent/A Rocha Conference, *Creation Groaning, Down to Earth Gospel*. Vancouver, BC, 2003.
Leopold, Aldo. *A Sand County Almanac*. Oxford: Oxford University Press, 1949.
Berry, Wendell. *Collected Poems*. New York: North Point, 1995.

CHAPTER FOUR: A FAMILY OF CRACKED POTS

Brown Taylor, Barbara. *An Altar in the World*. New York: Harper Collins, 2009.
Sacks, Jonathan. *The Dignity of Difference*. New York: Continuum, 2002.

CHAPTER FIVE: NAMING, NOT CLAIMING

IUCN Red List of Threatened Species. Online: http://www.iucn.org/.

CHAPTER SIX: WINDOWS INTO WONDER

Bouma-Prediger, Steven. *For the Beauty of the Earth*. Grand Rapids: Baker Academic, 2010.
Louv, Richard. *Last Child in the Woods: Saving our Children from Nature-Deficit Disorder*. Chapel Hill, NC: Algonquin, 2008.
Postman, Neil. *Amusing Ourselves to Death: Public Discourse in an Age of Entertainment*. New York: Penguin, 1985.
The Quiz, "Where on Earth Are You?" was adapted by Loren and Mary Ruth Wilkinson in *Caring for Creation in Your Own Backyard* (Vancouver, BC: Regent College Publishing, 1997) from Bill Durvall and George Sessions, *Deep Ecology*. Layton, UT: Gibbs Smith, 1985.

CHAPTER SEVEN: MINDFUL MEALS

Pollan, Michael. *The Omnivore's Dilemma: A Natural History of Four Meals*. New York: Penguin, 2007.

CHAPTER EIGHT: RESCUING THE OX FROM THE WELL

Snyder, Gary. *Practice of the Wild*. New York: North Point, 1990.
Pollan, Michael. *The Omnivore's Dilemma: A Natural History of Four Meals*. New York: Penguin, 2007.
Rollin, Bernard. "Farm Factories." In *Food & Faith: Justice, Joy and Daily Bread*. Edited by Michael Schut. Denver: Living the Good News, 2002.
Proceedings of the National Academy of Sciences. Online: November 3, 2008. http://news.ucdavis.edu/search/news detail.lasso?id=8983.

CHAPTER NINE: LIVING JUSTLY, LOVING MERCY, WALKING HUMBLY

Simiyu, Stella. "Perspectives." A lecture delivered at the Regent College/A Rocha Conference, *Keeping Earth in Common: A Just Faith for a Whole World.* Vancouver, BC, 2006.

Merkel, Jim. *Radical Simplicity.* Gabriola Island, BC: New Society, 2003.

Schlosser, Eric. *Fast Food Nation: The Dark Side of the All American Meal.* New York: Houghton Mifflin, 2001.

Food Inc. A documentary directed by Robert Kenner. Magnolia Pictures, 2008.

Lappe, Anna. *Diet for a Hot Planet.* New York: Bloomsbury, 2010.

Pollan, Michael. *The Omnivore's Dilemma: A Natural History of Four Meals.* New York: Penguin, 2007.

Peters, Christian J., et al. "Testing a Complete-Diet Model for Estimating the Land Resource Requirements of Food Consumption and Agricultural Carrying Capacity: The New York State Example." In *Renewable Agriculture and Food Systems* 22, no. 2, 2007.

Manufactured Landscapes. A documentary by Jennifer Baichwal and Edward Burtnysky. Foundry Films, 2007.

Brown, Edward. *Our Father's World: Mobilizing the Church to Care for Creation.* Downer's Grove, IL: InterVarsity, 2006.

McKibben, Bill. *Eaarth.* New York: Knopf, 2010.

Spencer, Nick, et al. *Christianity, Climate Change, and Sustainable Living.* Peabody, MA: Hendrickson, 2009.

CHAPTER TEN: EVERYTHING BUT THE SCHNITZEL

Berry, Wendell. "The Whole Horse." In *The Art of the Commonplace: The Agrarian Essays of Wendell Berry.* Berkeley, CA: Counterpoint, 2002.

Willard, Dallas. *The Divine Conspiracy.* New York: Harper Collins, 1998.

Foster, Richard. *Freedom of Simplicity.* New York: Harper Collins, 1981.

Berry, Wendell. "The Idea of a Local Economy. " In *Food & Faith: Justice, Joy and Daily Bread.* Edited by Michael Schut. Denver: Living the Good News, 2002.

Jordan, Chris. *Intolerable Beauty: Portrait of American Mass Consumption* . No pages. Online: http: //www.chrisjordan.com/.

Leddy, Mary Jo. *Radical Gratitude.* Maryknoll, NY: Orbis, 2002.

Heschel, Abraham Joshua. *The Sabbath.* New York: Farrar, Straus and Giroux, 1951.

CHAPTER TWELVE: CRADLING CREATION

The last line, ". . .choose joy though we've considered all the facts," alludes to Wendell Berry's poem, "Manifesto: The Mad Farmer Liberation Front." *Collected Poems*. New York: North Point, 1995.